Learning
Disabilities
and Games

Learning Disabilities and Games

Sophie L. Lovinger, Ph.D

Illustrations by Shurle Lee

Nelson Hall/Chicago

Library of Congress Cataloging in Publication Data

Lovinger, Sophie L
  Learning disabilities and games.

  Bibliography: p.
  Includes index.
  1. Play. 2. Child development. 3. Games.
4. Learning disabilities. 5. Perceptual-motor learning.
I. Title.
LB1137.L7   155.4'18   78-24619
ISBN 0-88229-353-2 (cloth)
ISBN 0-88229-652-3 (paper)

Manufactured in the United States of America

10   9   8   7   6   5   4   3   2   1

Contents

This book is dedicated to all children and to all who once were children, but especially to Mark, Michael, Suzanne, Ilene, Barbara, and David.

The Land of Counterpane

When I was sick and lay a-bed
I had two pillows at my head,
And all my toys beside me lay
To keep me happy all the day.

And sometimes for an hour or so
I watched my leaden soldiers go,
With different uniforms and drills,
Among the bed-clothes, through the hills;

And sometimes sent my ships in fleets
All up and down among the sheets;
Or brought my trees and houses out,
And planted cities all about.

I was the giant great and still
That sits upon the pillow-hill
And sees before him, dale and plain,
The pleasant land of counterpane.

Robert Louis Stevenson

1 Play

* * * * *

There is a Chinese proverb that states

If I see, I forget
If I hear, I remember
If I do, I learn

The last line reflects the essence of learning for us all. As adults, we can think through a problem in our heads. We experiment with alternatives and arrive at a suitable solution. Children do not have this ability and hence experiment with alternatives and solve their dilemmas via imaginative play and games.

That games and playing are learning experiences for children often comes as a surprise to adults. When we are particularly involved in some work of our own, and our children ask questions, we more often than not ask them to go out and play. On the other hand, when we wish them to perform a chore or task, we tell them to stop playing and do the chore which will help them to develop a sense of responsibility. When children are slower than we expect them to be, we tell them to stop playing and do their jobs. In other words, games and playing are a diversion and not very important. After all, don't we play when we go on vacation? It is a breather from work, it's relaxation, and it's fun, while work is serious and important, too. Children do not work, except as adults define school as work; they merely play, and that is not important.

Unfortunately we as adults all too often forget what it was like being a child and having what seemed like the whole adult world ordering us around, defining what was good and proper and important and what was not, without consulting us or trying to understand. We have forgotten what it felt like to have no power to counter adults and to always "have to" listen. We have forgotten what playing and games meant to us, that in them, we tried to deal with the adult world.

The following discussions of playing and games may jog your memories of those long forgotten times. We will start with the basic idea that playing, for children, is a very serious business. Dr. Clark Moustakas (1975) reminds us: "Of the many challenges that children face in their relations with parents and other significant adults, none is more devastating than the continual experience of not being listened to, not being recognized or understood. Repeated failure to communicate effectively one's own feelings, preferences, desires, and thoughts inevitably leads to frustration and doubts about one's value as a person" (p. 1).

Misunderstanding is inevitable between two people. As adults we fantasize what we would do or say if we had the chance to do it again. Children make believe and play games as a way of reestablishing the felt loss of esteem.

Children lack real power and must, therefore, comply with the demands and expectations of the adult world. Games and playing help children cope with the pressures of these demands and expectations.

Jimmy, a third grader, was in conflict with his teacher. He told stories to protect himself when he was caught doing something that broke the rules of the classroom. He preferred to chat with the other children rather than do his reading assignments, a task he did well, but which he was not particularly interested in doing; math was his area of interest and strength. After weeks of difficulties with the teacher, Jimmy was hard at work making two books. In one was a series of simple addition problems. The other book, entitled "Teachers Edishun," had the problems worked out. He explained to his mother that a friend was having trouble with math. He was making the first book so that his friend could practice and learn how to add. Then he was going to give his friend the second book to check his work.

In this instance, Jimmy was taking on the characteristics of the teacher. In make believe, as the teacher, he could do all the things the teacher could, and by way of this identification, could comply with her demands, something he was not able to do in reality. Jimmy included two important pieces of information in his play. One, he told himself that as he became more like grownups, he would be better able to meet their demands. Two, he communicated to the adult that much as he needed to do things on his own, he still needed the help of adults to attain the goals they set for him. This incident points up that playing helps children cope with pressures from adults and is a shortcut to learning about the world, oneself, and how one functions. It helps children learn about their strengths and weaknesses. It is also a way of learning how to be responsible for oneself, how to get along with one's peers, the rules and regulations of interpersonal relationships, winning, losing, taking one's turn, competing, cooperating, risking, eye-hand coordination, position in space, spatial relationships, form constancy, alphabetic sequencing, number concepts, arithmetic, and geography. The list seems endless.

Recently, I watched a little girl of six who was jumping in place and using two kinds of remarkably complicated foot movements in a repetitive fashion. She usually engaged in this activity while waiting for an adult to finish what he or she was doing. When the child was asked what she was doing, she answered in such a manner as to suggest that the question was a silly one. She explained that one of the foot movements was hop scotch jumps, which she was practicing, while the other set of movements was jump rope steps, which she could do at any time and didn't even need a rope. This response was from a child who was quite clumsy and uncoordinated, who had had so many accidents that her mother was convinced she would not live long enough to grow up. That she practiced these steps in her spare moments and in spite of her clumsiness underscores the importance of games and the skills involved. Games provide children with a remediation program of their own.

A number of years ago I worked with an optometrist in conjunction with children with perceptual problems and learning disabilities. He said that when he was in school he and some of his fellow students took a trip around New York City in search of groups of children playing the games he remembered playing on the streets of New York as a child. He could not find groups of playing children anywhere. His story reminded me of a trip to Boston where I found a group of boys sitting on their knees in the middle of a street watching carefully as a member of their group shot a marble into a cluster of marbles in the center of a circle marked on the ground. I felt excited, for I hadn't seen a group of children playing for a long time. As these games have dropped out of the repertoire of children, there has been increasing concern on the part of educators about the high incidence of learning disabilities.

It has been hypothesized that children with learning disabilities have minimal brain dysfunction, that is, brain damage not discernible on any medical assessment, but which may be related to some as yet undiscovered bio-chemical dysfunction. However, in the United States it is estimated that up to forty percent of school age children suffer from this syndrome. That the rest of the world experiences this phenomenon in only one percent of school age children suggests that something is amiss.

We are a country that emphasizes a high level of aca-demic achievement at the expense of a great many other goals. This concern is transmitted to our children. Since achievement is so important, play must be relegated to times when children are not engaged in anything more "meaningful" or more "important." Yet some of the remediation techniques in the area of learning disabilities used by Frostig, Kephart, Dolman-Delacatto, and others, have as their basis an emphasis on sensory-motor skills, upon which games and playing have their foundations. In a sense, these remediation techniques are taking the place of the games that children used to play.

One of the remediation techniques often used is a bal-ance beam, a plank of wood approximately one foot by five feet on a stand. Children practice walking across the board without falling off as a means of remediating coordination. Most mothers and fathers could tell you that their young children walk on all ledges within their ability to climb. Part of the fun is in being taller than the adult and part is in being able to walk that narrow ledge without falling off.

The older child can be seen walking along the curb between the sod and the street, arms outstretched, balanc-ing himself, and noting how far he had come before he lost balance. Given a chance, children practice the skill of balance-beam walking in many informal ways.

The optometrist mentioned previously used a balance beam as part of his training. Recently, he told me that while he still uses the balance beam, he no longer directs a child's activity upon it. Rather, he puts the child in a room with the balance beam and lets the child do his own thing. The optometrist stated that this gives better results than when the child is directed by an adult. Remediation techniques, which attempt to make a linkage between two or more of the sense modalities, cannot fully take the place of the rich complexity of children's games. The latter not only link up a multiplicity of sense modalities but also add to feelings of competence in peer relationships and feelings of self-worth in relationship to handling the rules of the game well. A remediation technique cannot generate these feelings as it is aimed at pointing out one's short-comings and is so devised as to make one's weaknesses stronger. Overtly, games do not attempt to do anything but provide a child with a fun situation, where just playing the game feels good, whether he wins or loses. A remediation technique subjugates the child to the adult; in playing a game, a child can be an active, assertive group member. Sensory-motor remediation techniques seem to point out that there is an area of experience necessary if a child is to develop a variety of skills. Before I begin to describe games, their teachings, and how they can be used in a remediation program for learning-disabled children, we should look at what play means to children.

The first game most children play is Peek-a-boo. Parents usually initiate this game when a baby is four to five months of age. The first attempt at this game usually frightens the child: the world has suddenly disappeared. When the world reappears there is a noticeable excitement, giggling, and squirming on the child's part. After a while, the child can play the game on his own initiative and with variations. The child is learning from this simple game that he can make the world disappear and can also make it reappear on his own initiative.

To many people, this interpretation may seem far-fetched. However, think back to the last time you played with a five-month-old baby. If you were wearing glasses, dangling earrings, or a necklace, or had a pen in your pocket, the baby made a grab for the object. When you removed the object from the baby's sight, the baby looked at the place where it was. When it was gone, the baby looked for something else to play with, as if the object no longer existed. If you cover a baby's eyes, the world no longer is there.

Five months later in the life of the child, there is a different response. Take the object away from the baby and he will follow your movements and seek the object where he saw you hide it. This suggests that the baby senses that objects exist independent of his or her ability to see them. This knowledge helps the baby learn that the world is a stable and constant place.

All children have the experience of being deserted. Being put down for a nap and the adult leaving the room gives rise to feelings of desertion. The child must passively accept what is being done to her or him. Many psychologists agree that one of the first developmental tasks an infant must master is passivity. The infant must move from being a passive receiver of ministrations to an active participant in the child-rearing process. The movement from passivity to activity can be seen by the time a baby has learned to crawl. If an adult puts a baby on the floor to play and then leaves the room, more often than not the baby begins to cry. However, if the adult remains in the room and the baby crawls out, he will not cry. The baby does not have to passively accept the important adult leaving. He can leave the adult when he wants to and yet have the adult back (by crawling back into the room) when he so desires.

The child begins to learn at an early age that he does not have to be at the mercy of others, that he can do things and make things happen on his own initiative. This knowledge leads to a feeling of competence, a feeling of "I can do it all by myself." Very important lessons are learned by the child from this simple game begun in infancy. (That Peek-a-boo is important is reflected in the increasingly sophisticated forms of the theme found throughout childhood: Hide and Seek, secret clubs, playing in a tree house, or standing behind a door to say "Boo" to startle someone coming in.)

Games and playing seem to have three distinct phases. The first is make-believe, which is basically seen until children are six or seven years of age. The second is beginning team games, where the children argue about rules and regulations more than they actually play, which ranges from age six until about eight or nine. Third are team games which start at about age nine and last through college and beyond (for example, professional baseball, football, basketball, and soccer).

Make-believe is the earliest interactive game form children use to practice skills and to understand the things that they are learning day by day. The make-believe play with which we are most familiar begins at about the time the baby reaches his or her first birthday. At this time, the child does to the adult what has been experienced by the child. For example, the child will feed the adult with a spoon as the adult is feeding the child, or the child will brush the adult's hair as the adult is brushing the child's hair.

By eighteen months of age, the child can transfer these activities to a doll—feeding it, rocking it, putting it to sleep. The child will also dust, make beds, cook, sweep, phone, and imitate a variety of other behaviors that have been observed.

A favorite blanket or toy often becomes an important member of the family by the time a child is two. My own son had his "blanket" which was separate from the covers he used when he went to sleep. The blanket loved to be cuddled, and sit on his shoulder. Upon occasion, the

blanket sat at the table, on its own chair, with its own
dishes and tableware and had dinner with the family.

In a child one to two years of age, we see a progression
from simple imitation of adults to caring for a doll to
an imaginary type of communication with a less representational item, such as my son's blanket. The first stage
in the development of play, imitation of the adult, grows
in complexity. This imitative play moves from the "real"
situation, in which the copied behaviors usually occur
(for example, feeding done at the kitchen table), to novel
settings (feeding the doll under the bed).

In play, the child copies, imitates, and finally identifies
with those adults in the environment that are of crucial
importance to him. While the child initially only repro-
duces the ordinary caretaking routines, the pleasure in the
play arises from voluntary involvement, actively doing the
activity, and mastering the behaviors. The child in the
play situation is the active doer rather than the passive
receiver. These aspects of play lead one to the conclusion
that through play children master and organize their
understanding of the world, which they obtain from their
relationships with others.

By the time a child is three, play is also a means whereby
he or she comes to grips with what it means to be a boy
or girl. Children learn the appropriate social role for their
sex through the handling they receive from their parents
and significant others and also by identification. Identification is a process whereby the child decides that he or
she wants to be like the important person he has chosen.
This most often is, at first, the parent of the same sex.
The characteristics the child chooses are those that say
to the child "Here is a competent person." By taking on
those characteristics viewed as competent, the child, in
turn, can consider himself competent.

Other important people of the same sex are also identi-
fied with, for example, a police officer or a teacher. The

teacher helps children to learn, tells them what to do while they listen, and takes care of children. Little girls and boys try out being the teacher, whom they see as competent, and by virtue of doing the same things as the teacher, take on for themselves the competencies they see the teacher possessing. Boys and girls, acting as they see police officers act, take on the competencies they see the police officers as possessing, which in turn makes them competent as people.

Make-believe, then, helps in the identification process by allowing the child to try on these aspects of competence she or he notices in the important people in the environment and thereby acquire those competencies.

Play and make-believe also help a child learn about the world. Playful exploration of a toy's versatility helps children begin to understand how things work, what toys can do, and what they can do to toys. They then transfer this information to the realm of interpersonal relationships. In doing things to and with people, the child gains a greater understanding of relationships. Testing out behaviors on objects and people helps the child confirm that he or she is a competent person, that people listen to him or her, that he or she is respected as a person. (This is one of the ways in which a child learns to respect others.) Building, making things, and putting things together are other play and make-believe activities which further the child's understanding of the world.

We can all agree that a child must learn these things. But why does it have to be through play? Through play, the child is able to bring the world down to manageable proportions. We too often forget that the concept of "giant" comes from the child and represents the real difference in size between the child and adults. An experiment was done in which a grown man used chairs, tables, and utensils that were as large proportional to his size as these things normally are to young children. He struggled to get up on the chair. When he finally sat down, he was unable to reach the table. Sitting on his knees gave him a more comfortable perch. While this man was well acquainted with the use of a knife and fork, they were so large that it was more efficient for him to pick up his food with his fingers. Reaching for objects on the table was difficult. The table was so large that he was unable to scan it quickly to find where different objects were placed. Food was spilt and objects were knocked off the table. This experiment focuses our attention on the difficulties small children have with adult-sized furniture and equipment. The toys of children are appropriate to their size, so as they play with them, they develop the skills and competencies to deal with the world as it is.

Cowboys and Indians is one of the games children play as a means of coming to grips with the meaning of death and dying, a concern of five-year-olds. If you shoot someone with your gun, what happens? Can he or she move? Breathe? Talk? Can a person come alive again? What does it feel like to be dead? This type of game is one way the young child has of understanding a difficult concept, hard even for adults to grasp.

Another form of make-believe is trying alternative modes of solving a problem. A little boy of five who had just been spanked by his mother for a misdemeanor made believe he was talking to his father on the phone. He told him that his mother had hit him. He was quiet for a few seconds as though listening to the response, shook his head, then said, "Uh huh, I should hit her back!" The child protested that his mother might hit him in return, listened once again to the make-believe voice, then asked, "Should I hit mommy and then run away?" Again there was a protestation that mother would just catch him and hit him in return. The child listened some more and then commented that he should tell his mother that he did not like being hit and that he was mad at her. The child discussed with himself what he would like to do, solved the dilemma of the inappropriateness of that form of behavior, and then decided how he would deal with his feelings. His solution was clearly most helpful to him, encouraged him to share his feelings with his mother, and led him to the knowledge that it was all right to be angry with her. This seems a pretty good way to solve a problem—looking at one's feelings and the alternative ways in which one can deal with them in the real world.

The above discussion covers briefly the meaning of young children's play and games. Playing teaches children important lessons about themselves and the world that can be learned only by doing. These lessons cannot be learned when the child is a passive participant—when he is told how to do it, what to do, or just that it is done. He or she has to be actively involved in the activity for it to make sense. This is especially so up to about seven years of age, when a child learns most effectively by doing.

By six or seven, the child has a good sense of being a boy or a girl and some basic information about what is appropriate behavior for each sex. The issue of identification becomes less crucial. The concern that comes into sharp focus at this time revolves about the child's ability to take care of himself or herself without constant supervision. This concern coincides with school entrance, especially during first grade. Mother and father are no longer ever-present. The child can no longer depend upon the status of his parents to establish his own status. He or she must now find a place in the world through achievement.

Since one cannot lean upon one's parents within the school, and they are not around to remind one of rules and regulations, one must be able to use the rules and regulations already learned. At this time, rules and regulations become a very important aspect of functioning. A feeling of security is enhanced in children by their learning to work together in team games. They learn to function according to rules and regulations and to behave in ways appropriate to their sex. At this time, the boy who does not behave as boys are expected to and the girl who does not behave as girls are expected to are often the outcasts of the group. The group reinforces appropriate behavior, and helps children conform to rules and regulations.

Charles Schultz, in his comic strip "Peanuts," characterized this period beautifully when he portrayed the arguments the gang had on the pitcher's mound. Games during this period, then, involve arguments about the rules of play more than actual playing together. Rules are rigid and no deviation is tolerated. Severe, unusual, and sometimes inhuman treatment is meted out for infractions of the rules. Because children at this time of their lives are not certain of what is appropriate, right and wrong, or good and bad in game playing, they cannot allow deviations. This is not to say that there is no game playing, but rather that the most obvious feature is arguments. Through arguing, children learn that they can deal with rules and regulations by themselves, that they have really learned what is right and wrong and which skills they possess. They finally come to grips with whatever competencies they have developed, while slowly developing others. It is the feeling of competence that allows children to take chances in areas where they are not sure of their skills.

The third phase of game playing allows for minor infractions of rules, changing rules to suit special needs of the children and of the game, and developing games with sets of rules and regulations. This phase further enhances feelings of competence. Team spirit, working together, and helping one another along can occur only after children have been able to test out abilities and disabilities and find out what they can do and what is beyond their abilities. Play at this level of development is a way of practicing a variety of skills within a social context where there is both cooperation and competition. Nevertheless, underlying most children's games are the goals of competence and self-worth, which can be obtained only through active interaction with the world.

With an increasing reliance on television and on toys that require only the pushing of a button, passivity has been encouraged. Little effort is needed to watch the television screen or to push a button and have the toy move. Television undermines activity and tends to create children who demand that things be easy and handed to them with little effort on their part. This is not to say the TV does not have its place. But it is not a replacement for spontaneous play. Play requires the player to be an active participant, the mover of the toy, the creator of the scene and the action. The child becomes the script writer, the producer, the director, and the actor all at the same time. Children are active organisms who learn actively.

In the following section are a series of games that children used to play. Along with the plans of the games, chants are included, as well as what these games teach the children (which underscores their importance).

As I talked to people about the games they used to play when they were children, I sensed that they were excited about these childhood experiences. Invariably, they commented that they do not see children playing these games anymore and they wondered why, for the games were so much fun.

2   Who's Gonna Be "It"

*   *   *   *   *

The beginnings of games are almost as important as the games themselves. In play, children decide upon the game and how it will be played, set up the ground rules, and then carry the play through to completion. They assume the responsibility for the total organization of the activity from beginning to end. We, as adults, frequently wish to instill in our children a sense of responsibility, especially when it entails the completion of a job. We will discuss later why this occurs when children play games. Now we will concern ourselves with how it all begins.

Sometimes when a game is named, children quickly call out "Not It." The child who is unfortunate enough to call out last is automatically "It." On the other hand, if turns are necessary for the playing of the game, the children call out "First," "Second," "Third," and so on, and order themselves. This is the simplest way of beginning the game. Another alternative, preferred by some, allows the child who suggested the game to choose who goes first, who belongs to what team, or who is "It." This is often accomplished by a ritualized chant.

Most of the time, more than one child will name the same game. How, then, is the caller chosen? One child may call out "Odds," the other, "Evens." They stand facing one another, shaking their fists while chanting, "One,

18

two, three, shoot," whereupon they put out one or two fingers. If the total count of fingers is an odd number, the child who called "Odds" racks up a point. If the total count of fingers is an even number, the child who called "Evens" racks up a point. (This calling of odds and evens helps a child understand some mathematical facts.) The children decide whether one takes it, or two out of three, three out of five, and so on. The winner of this play becomes the chooser.

When three children are involved, calling odds and evens won't work. They may choose with fingers too, however. The children stand in a circle, call, "One, two, three, shoot," and put out their fingers. The child whose fingers do not match the others is eliminated in this play. The remaining two children call odds and evens and proceed as before.

When four children are involved, two pairs of odds and evens will choose for the winner, with the winners choosing again.

The "chooser" decides on a chant. The children may stand in a circle or on a line; more often they crowd around one another, arms extended, hands in a fist. The chooser lightly taps each fist with his or her own, reciting a chant as he taps each fist. The fist that receives a tap on the last word of the chant is put behind the owner's back. The child who has both hands behind his back is out—he or she is not "It." The chanting continues until one child is left. That child becomes "It." Following is a chant I recall from my childhood:

> *Bubble gum, bubble gum, in a dish*
> *How many pieces do you wish?*

[the child whose fist is tapped picks a number from one to ten and counts out the number on the fists available, ending with]

> *And you're not it!* [or]
> *And you are it!*

How this chant ends depends on whether the chooser likes a child or not. Not knowing which line is to be used heightens the suspense of the players.

Some cheating may be done by splitting the word into syllables and giving each syllable a tap, or by combining two words and giving one tap; but this is perfectly acceptable to children. As they are not sure about syllables and often slur two words together, they do not view this maneuver as cheating. And, since it's the children's game and their form of choosing, they need to manage it by themselves.

Here are a few more chants:

> Blue shoe, blue shoe
> How old are you?
> One, two, three, four?
> It is you!
>
> *   *   *
>
> Inka, binka, bottle of ink
> The cork fell out and you stink
> Not because you're dirty
> Not because you're clean
> Just because you kissed a boy
> Behind the magazine.
>
> *   *   *
>
> Eeny, meeny, miny, moe
> Catch a piggie by the toe
> If he hollers
> Let him go
> Eeny, meeny, miny, moe
> My mother said to pick this one
> And out goes Y-O-U
>
> *   *   *
>
> One potato, two potato,
> Three potato, four
> Five potato, six potato
> Seven potato, more
>
> *   *   *

Intery, mintery, cutery, corn
Apple seed and apple thorn
Wire, briar, limber lock
How many geese to make a flock?
One flew east, and one flew west
One flew over the cuckoo's nest.

     *   *   *

Icka, bicka, balinda
The monkey washed the winda
The winda broke
The monkey got soaked
Icka, bicka, balinda.

     *   *   *

One, two, three
Mother caught a flea
Flea died, mother cried
One, two, three.

     *   *   *

Dickery, dickery, dare
The pig flew up in the air
The man in brown
Soon brought him down
Dickery, dickery, dare.

     *   *   *

Monkey in the matchbox
Don't you hear him holler
Take him to the station house
And make him pay a dollar.

The chant below is accomplished, not by tapping fists, but by tapping on the toes of the children.

Engine, engine number nine
Going down Chicago line
If the train falls off the track
Do you want your money back?

The child whose toes are tapped answers either yes or no. The word is then spelled out by tapping on the shoes available and in order. The chant then continues.

> *And you are not it!* [or]
> *And you are it.*

The elaborate rituals of choosing, as described above, certainly can be accomplished more efficiently if an adult intervenes and makes the choices for the children. It would also seem to the adult that he can expedite the play more fairly, too. I am reminded of a third-grade teacher who wished to run a democratic classroom. As one way of facilitating this, she arranged for an election of class officers by the students. Once this had been accomplished, she discussed with the group the necessity for leaving the room in an orderly fashion, and such issues as safety, orderliness, the need for quiet so that other classes could work, and her responsibility for all the children. She then charged the group to decide on ways they could meet the needs just discussed. The children went off to solve the problem while she worked at her desk.

Although this teacher did not describe what method the children devised, she said that it was a rather complex procedure, where the children neither lined up by size, nor separated themselves on the basis of sex. However, she did not have to remind the children about noise or pushing or keeping together; the children reminded themselves. They had devised the rules and abided by them; it was their responsibility.

Think back to the last time someone told you how to do something that you carried through, and later tried on your own in your own way. Which was the more effective and efficient way? How do you feel when someone demands that you do something his way and you have your own ideas about how it should be done? Children learn what are the best ways for them if they are given the opportunities to find out. By deciding for children, we deprive them of basic experiences. Deciding upon the game and the manner of its organization helps children learn self-determination and responsibility. This leads to their feeling that they are capable of ordering and organizing their own lives, independent of adults.

When Mark was eight, his favorite choosing chant was "Bubble gum, bubble gum in a dish." He used it to decide what he was going to eat first, what shirt he would like his mother to buy, and what candies he would like to purchase with his allowance. It was apparent from his behavior that he had made his choice before using the chant, for if the chant was completed upon the wrong item, he would rechant until the right item was chosen. Clearly he was not sure of his decision-making abilities and could fob off a bad choice on the chance factors of the chant. Mark used chants for a long time. At ten, more certain of his ability to make good decisions, he dispensed with them.

Fairness, which is always an issue with children, must be considered from their point of view, rather than from our viewpoint. Their notions of fairness are very different from an adult's. We would probably, at times, call their approach cruel, but children accept the evaluations of their peers more readily than those of adults who are considered to be "enemies" who "don't understand."

In the previous chapter we said that during their early school years, children are concerned about rules and regulations, right and wrong, and good and bad. They cannot depend on their parents for a reminder while they are in school and hence must depend upon their own memory. Choosing rituals helps them to structure their lives, to learn more fully the rules and regulations of living within a social group. The choosing rituals supplement the instructions of teachers and parents and help the children assume responsibility for their games. Rituals also allow them to experience and live with their own choices. If they are satisfied with what has happened, they will repeat the procedure. If they are dissatisfied, they can change it the next time. Isn't this the beginning of responsibility?

None of this, of course, diminishes the responsibility of the adult to introduce game playing at appropriate times and for specific group needs.

Everyone has a need for play. One of the ways this need can be satisfied, even in a classroom, is through the playing of games. Games can be used for: socializing; unifying the group (especially when it is composed of subgroups) ; release of energy; bringing out natural leadership or other special abilities of individuals; presenting new educational ideas; giving group members needed prestige; and helping children to remediate deficit sensory areas. The leader or teacher can use games to: study group members to better help them to be leaders; study adjustment problems; motivate various activities; study the learning capacities and limitations of the individual and the group; and channel impulses and ideas. The leader of a game must be thoroughly prepared in terms of the procedure and rules of the game. He or she must know the age, sex, physical size, and interests of the children, and the emotional status of the group at the moment (passive, submissive, tense, angry) .

The slow child (either physically or mentally), the chubby child, the physically disabled child, and the child with glasses are often not chosen by other children to participate in games or are unable to compete in the games. The leader needs to keep the abilities and disabilities of all the children in mind, but especially those of the handicapped children of the group. The leader could use team games where the weaknesses are not obvious as well as incorporating noncompetitive games into the play session. Singling out the handicapped child for special treatment only emphasizes the disability. Using a game where the handicap is minimized would be the more helpful approach. As group leader, you should emphasize the strengths of a child.

In any group there is typically the shy, inhibited child

who needs to become involved in his own way, at his own rate. The leader must be alert to the cues a child expresses regarding his interests. Games the shy child seems interested in can be introduced to draw this type of child into group activities.

When a "tie" occurs, the leader should allow the group to decide how it wishes to resolve the problem. The group might replay the game, or settle the decision by lot or by another game.

Sometimes there are fights between individual group members. If it is a serious fight, the leader must realize that emotions must be exhausted before members can be reasoned with, then find out the reason for the fight. Individuals can be taken to the gym to settle the fight by rules of fair play (boxing or a competitive game). The individuals should be given the responsibility for carrying out the activity.

The autocratic group member needs help in channeling his need for leadership in a constructive manner. This can be accomplished by helping the autocratic child present games and activities to the rest of the group democratically. Rules of the game can be covered, and team games can be emphasized.

Games should be stopped just after the peak of interest and excitement has been reached, and the group smoothly moved into a new activity.

3 Peek-a-Boo and Others of Its Ilk

★ ★ ★ ★ ★

Perceptual skills are necessary for learning. Perceptual skills, in this context, refers to all of the sense modalities: seeing, hearing, touching, tasting, and smelling. The skill aspect of perception is based on coordinations and/or integrations of all the sense modalities.

Perception is a process, beginning at birth, of organizing and interpreting the sensations that arise in the body and that come through the various sense organs. The child is continually perceiving. From the earliest days of infancy he or she squirms or thrashes away from a source of irritation, cries in response to hunger, and calms down at the sound of mother's voice. Later, the sound of words or the appearance of specific objects act as a stimulus for perception. In preschool and grade school years, the sights, sounds, smells, and other features of the environment are the sources of perceptions which lead to thinking. Perception, then, is the beginning of thinking. Children and adults alike learn about things by observing them. Without perception a child would have no memories and no imagination, which would result in little or no learning occurring. Observation is not sufficient for learning, however. Touching, lifting, hearing, shoving, and climbing are all experiences that enhance learning and become co-

ordinated with visual perception. These experiences form
the basis for understanding the facts of the environment
as well as for generalizing about them in the form of concepts and problem solving. The first concepts that develop
seem to be those relating to size, form, and color, and are
the basis of knowledge about the world upon which attitudes, beliefs, and values are constructed.

The raw materials of perception and thinking are sensations. A sensation is an awareness of some stimulus without much interpretation. For example, when you are
deeply involved in the plot of a novel, it may take you a
few moments to be aware of a doorbell ringing. So, in
addition to five basic senses of seeing, hearing, smelling,
touching, and tasting are the sensations of position and
movement, color, tones, and so on. Keep in mind, however, that sensations seldom exist as isolated phenomena.
The child interprets and integrates them to form percepts.

From sensations and percepts of related data a concept
is usually organized which is nearly always a verbal sym-
bol. This generalization about the available data reflects
the child's understanding of the world. In turn, the concept assists the child in clarifying his or her experiences
and giving meaning to them. While sensations and percepts arise within the body of the infant, the second set of
sensations and percepts arise via the relation of child to
environment. This is accomplished through vision.

Vision seems to be the first modality developed. The
twelve tiny eye muscles of the newborn are the most developed parts of the body, which allows for the early differentiation of this modality. According to Piaget (1952),
the other sense modalities are linked to the visual. For a
long time the infant just looks at anything that comes
within its visual field. This looking gives one the impression that the infant is devouring objects with its eyes. As
the infant matures, integrations develop between looking
and hearing, looking and grasping, grasping and tasting.

Since with grasp and taste the infant brings the object close to its face, smelling becomes coordinated with tasting, grasping, seeing, and hearing. All of these integrations and intercoordinations occur within the first four to five months of life and are practiced and refined thereafter.

To the infant each object seen is completely new; for a long time, objects cannot be generalized to classes of objects. For instance, to the young baby, three differently shaped rattles are three distinct objects rather than a class of toys to be shaken to make noise. If an object is seen rightside up, looking at it upside down makes it another object.

Psychologists have understood this phenomenon as a lack of object constancy. In other words, objects have no permanence. Once they are out of the visual field, they cease to exist. For the young infant there is no reality, space, time, or permanence; there are only events which have no relationship to what has previously occurred or to what comes next. Gradually, towards the middle of the first year of life, the infant begins to make differential responses to objects, showing preferences for some and disinterest in others. Concurrent with this beginning memory of an object is the recognition of the mother as an important person in the life of the infant. Consistent mothering as well as the games mothers play with their babies help the infant to develop the object constancy necessary to function adequately in the world.

Peek-a-boo is one of these first games. Through this game the infant learns that he can make the world disappear and come back at will. Most importantly, he does not have to be at the mercy of people who can leave him. In addition to the development of object constancy, a sense of competence in making the world disappear and reappear at will begins. The child with a reading disability often seems to be lacking some form of object-constancy. He or she can read a word in one sentence but often does not know what the word is when it occurs in another sentence. It is almost as if the differing configurations of the two sentences automatically means to the child that the words must be different.

When the child does not develop the concept of object-constancy, the world remains a rather confusing place. As long as confusion reigns, a child can gain little sense of his abilities in similar situations. Feelings of incompetence rather than competence are generated.

We said previously that games encourage feelings of competence in children. Children who are failing in academic work have a seriously undermined sense of competence which often undercuts their ability to learn. These feelings of inadequacy and shame in relationship to teachers and peers propel a child to hide, and the child tends to be resistant to learning. This child is often the class clown or the class behavior problem. In a sense, the unacceptable behaviors which cover an underlying feeling of incompetence enable the child to be recognized for competence in some area, even if the behaviors are detrimental. The child who becomes what we call "learning disabled" comes to school with the knowledge that his or her body does not function as he wishes, that he feels ill-equipped to survive emotionally and psychologically in the environment.

Concomitant with this is a poor concept of self, a negative self-image, and a history of failure. The child who has failed to master the standards and expectations set for him by the important adults in the environment has built into his self-concept the notion that he is a failure; upon entrance into the educational system he will function to maintain that concept and fail. That the child has failed to master parental standards and expectations because of his helplessness in controlling basic drives and impulses and in relating effectively to the world is no less

a potent force than when these failures are due to difficult parent-child relationships. Whereas, the child who is
in conflict with his parents may rebel against parental
standards and expectations, the learning disabled child, by
the very nature of his deficits, is unable to incorporate
them. The consequence is severe, chronic anxiety, which
is in itself disabling. The experiential aspect of chronic
anxiety is that of one's imminent death. Distractibility,
overreactivity, physical awkwardness, and temper out-
bursts are the child's attempts to get away from the over-
whelming sense of impending doom. However, peers cannot predict when or how the learning disabled child is
going to respond, nor can they understand what the child
is responding to in the environment. The learning disabled child, if a girl, does not respond as peers expect a
girl to respond, nor will a learning disabled boy respond
as peers expect. The child is then rejected by peers, further
intensifying feelings of failure and reinforcing the concept
of one's self as a failure.

The development of feelings of competence in areas not
related to academic work may generate enough courage
for the child to deal with those areas of difficulty previously avoided and thereby obtain recognition and acceptance. Games have this quality, especially if they are linked
in some way with the disability and have a training aspect
to them.

Variation of Peek-a-boo are the Hide and Seek games
which encourage and link the sense modalities, especially
the visual and auditory. In Hide and Seek proper, the
child who is "It" covers his or her eyes for a specific time
period ("It" may count to fifty or some other number the
group decides upon). Here the teacher could build in
number facts by having the child count to one hundred
by fives, tens, or threes. This counting should be within
the realm of what the child can accomplish without a

struggle to achieve; otherwise the object of the game has been destroyed before it has begun. The instructions to the group could be to make as much noise as possible so that the child who is "It" can tell where the sounds are coming from without too much difficulty. These rules can slowly be altered so that the group gradually moves from a maximum of noise to quiet. In this way, especially as the noise level decreases, the children must tune in to more and more subtle sounds, which may help sharpen auditory perception. The place where "It" covers his eyes is home base, a safe area to which a child who has been hiding can run before his or her name is called by "It." The player calls out "Home free" or "Home free all."

The child who is "It" often stands near home base, looking around carefully to spy the other players and call them out. This involves remembering what various children wore, which develops visual memory. The child who is "It" also has to develop strategies of looking and finding before the other children are aware of what is happening; the other children have to be on the lookout for the inattention of "It" so that they can reach home base before being tapped out. In essence much skill is called for in the playing of this game.

An alternate for Hide and Seek is a game called Sardines. In this game one child hides as the other children cover their eyes. Their task is to find the hider and join him. The last child then becomes the one who hides in the next round of the game. As more children find the hider, it becomes increasingly difficult for them to squeeze into the same place without being seen. The giggle level is hard to control, especially as excitement grows. Cooperation between the hiding children becomes crucial, for their pushing, activity, and noise make it much easier to find the hiding place.

Blind Man's Buff is another form of this game. The

child who is "It" is blindfolded and placed in the center of a circle formed by the rest of the children. They hold hands and skip around until the blindfolded child says "Stop." The "blind man" then points toward the perimeter of the circle, and the child pointed at moves into the circle with the blind man, but tries to keep away from him. If the blind man tags this child, he or she must stand still while the blind man touches his face and tries to guess who he is. One question may be asked by the blind man, but he cannot ask the name of the child. If the blind man guesses correctly, that child becomes the blind man. If not, the blind man continues as before.

The games described above require large playing areas such as a gym or playground and are not always appropriate for a classroom. A game that is quieter and appropriate for a classroom is Hot and Cold. Once again someone is "It." This child is sent out of the room while the rest of the group hides an object. Then "It" is invited back and has to search for the object. The rest of the group gives cues on the child's proximity to the object by shouting "Hot" or "Cold." Singing a song, either softly or loudly, can be substituted for shouting cold and hot.

Another game in this genre is Dog and Bone. One child plays the dog and sits on the ground, blindfolded, while the other players stand around him in a circle. Some object, called the "bone," is placed in front of him. One of the players approaches the bone quietly and attempts to steal it from the dog. If the player is heard, the dog says "Bow-wow" and points in the direction of the noise. The dog continues in his role until someone is successful in stealing the bone. Then the players on the perimeter of the circle say "Bow-wow." The successful robber then becomes the dog.

Carl, a little boy of six, had a great deal of difficulty distinguishing between himself and others. If another

child wore the same style and color pants he was wearing, Carl wondered whether he had become the other child or the other child had become him. Further, he wondered if the seats and desks were still in his classroom when he was not there. He clearly had not developed the notion of object constancy. In class, his teacher taught the group Dog and Bone. This game became Carl's favorite. He played it whenever he could with children and adults. The longer he played the game, the less Carl was confused about his own identity and the more he understood that people could be similar and yet different and that people and things existed even if he couldn't see them.

In all of these games, an "It" is needed; the choosing-chants described in the first chapter can be used to select someone for that role.

In our enthusiasm and desire to help the child with a learning disability, we must keep in mind that the disabled child should not always be chosen to be "It," nor should his or her turn at being "It" be neglected. Just playing the game gives each child the opportunity to take out of it whatever he needs at the moment. Taking turns should come as naturally for the disabled child as for other children. Bandura (1963), a psychologist who has investigated role modeling of children, has suggested that children can learn meaningful lessons from watching others. They do not always have to be active participants. The child playing Hide and Seek will listen to the various noises being made as carefully as the child who is "It," for he, too, wants to know where the other children are hiding. It gives him some ideas for hiding places the next time the game is played. A child also has to listen carefully to know when another child is running to home base; he learns when to leave his hiding place to tap home base without being caught or spotted before he wants to be.

Participating in these games calls into being feelings of being alive and active, of being in command of oneself and of the course of the game. In addition, the children learn that the world remains constant whether it can be seen or not. They also learn that they do not have to depend solely upon seeing to understand and know the world; they can depend also on their senses of touch and of hearing to gain meaningful information.

4   Pat-a-Cake

*   *   *   *   *

In the last chapter, we discussed the sense modalities (visual, auditory, tactile, taste, and smell) and the need for intercoordination between them. Tasting and smelling as means whereby the child gains information quickly are not as important as the other modalities. The major information gathering modalities of children are visual, auditory, and tactile. The tactile more than the visual and auditory requires physical activity. In addition to the sensations generated in the fingers when one touches an object or person is the comfort gained by being physically close to someone or something. In a sense, then, the tactile modality is important in interpersonal relationships.

Most of us are familiar with the following Mother Goose rhyme:

> *Pat-a-cake, pat-a-cake*
> *Baker's man,*
> *Bake me a cake*
> *As fast as you can.*
> *Pat it and prick it*
> *And mark it with a B,*
> *And put it in the oven*
> *For baby and me.*

This game, whether played by a mother and her baby or by two children, must be conducted face-to-face and involves cooperation and physical contact. In essence, it is a social game. In addition to the social value of this game, there is sensory-motor input. Chants are sung to Pat-a-Cake games which have a distinct rhythm. Hand movements must be coordinated with the beat of the chant and with the cadence of the other person clapping; it is a cooperative venture.

The contact inherent in these games should satisfy the learning disabled child's need to touch and at the same time should help him or her understand and appreciate his own strength; clapping too hard may hurt the other child, ruin the game, and exclude him from further participation. Some of these Pat-a-Cake games require complicated hand movements, which help children learn to concentrate on more than one thing at a time—the chant, the rhythm, how hard they are clapping, and what they have to do next with their hands. These games also help children develop the ability to cross over the midline of their bodies and to gain the concepts of right and left. This happens as the child's right hand faces the left hand of his partner in this face-to-face game; for right hands or left hands to clap, they must cross diagonally. Here are some chants that accompany these clapping games.

> *Miss Lucy had a baby*
> *She named him Tiny Tim*
> *She put him in a bathtub*
> *To see if he could swim.*
>
> *He drank up all the water*
> *He ate a bar of soap*
> *He tried to eat the bathtub*
> *But it wouldn't go down his throat*
>
> *Miss Lucy called the doctor*

The doctor called the nurse
The nurse called the lady
With the alligator purse.

"The measles," said the doctor
"The mumps," said the nurse
"Nothing," said the lady
With the alligator purse.

Then out walked the doctor
Then out walked the nurse
Then out walked the lady
With the alligator purse.

*   *   *   *   *

Granny, Granny, sick in bed
Called the doctor and the doctor said
"Granny, Granny, you ain't sick
All you need is a goodnight kiss."

*   *   *   *   *

When Billy Boy was one
He learned to suck his thumb
So thumbioka, thumbioka
When Billy Boy was one.

When Billy Boy was two
He learned to tie his shoe
So shoioka, shoioka
When Billy Boy was two.

When Billy Boy was three
He learned to touch his knee
So kneeioka, kneeioka
When Billy Boy was three.

When Billy Boy was four
He learned to touch the floor
[chorus]

When Billy Boy was five
He learned to reach the hive
[chorus]

When Billy Boy was six
He learned to pick up sticks
[chorus]

When Billy Boy was seven
He learned to count to eleven
[chorus]

When Billy Boy was eight
He opened the garden gate
[chorus]

When Billy Boy was nine
He learned to play quite fine
[chorus]

When Billy Boy was ten
He started all over again
[chorus]

Next is a Pat-a-Cake game that involves miming the motion mentioned, while at the same time keeping the rhythms of clapping and chanting.

A sailor went to sea, sea, sea [the children salute three
    times on the word *sea*]
To see [salute] *what he could see, see, see,* [salute]
But all that he could see, see, see [salute]
Was the bottom of the deep blue sea, sea, sea [salute].

A sailor went to chop, chop, chop [chopping motion
    on one arm three times]
To see [salute] *what he could chop, chop, chop*
    [chopping motion]
But all that he could chop, chop, chop [chopping motion]
Was the bottom of the deep blue chop, chop chop
    [chopping motion].

A sailor went to knee, knee, knee [touch knee three
    times]
To see [salute] *what he could knee, knee, knee*
    [touch knee]

But all that he could knee, knee, knee [touch knee]
Was the bottom of the deep blue knee, knee, knee
[touch knee]

A sailor went to toe, toe, toe [touch toe three times]
To see [salute] *what he could toe, toe, toe* [touch toe]
But all that he could toe, toe, toe [touch toe]

Was the bottom of the deep blue toe, toe, toe
[touch toe].

A sailor went to sea, chop, knee, toe [do all motions]
To see [salute] *what he could see, chop, knee, toe*
[all motions]

But all that he could see, chop, knee, toe [all motions]
Was the bottom of the deep blue sea, chop, knee, toe
[all motions].

The following Pat-a-Cake game uses complicated hand work. Each child claps his own hands, claps his partner's hands, crosses his arms to clap his shoulders, slaps his thighs, claps his hands, and then claps his partner's hands.

Miss Mary Mack, Mack, Mack
All dressed in black, black, black
With silver buttons, buttons, buttons
All down her back, back, back.

She asked her mother, mother, mother
For twenty-five cents, cents, cents
To see the elephant, elephant, elephant
Jump over the fence, fence, fence.

It jumped so high, high, high
It reached the sky, sky, sky
And didn't come down, down, down
'Til the Fourth of July, July, July.

Of course, there is always this old favorite:

Pease porridge hot
Pease porridge cold
Pease porridge in the pot
Nine days old.

Some like it hot
Some like it cold
Some like it in the pot
Nine days old.

Tactile and auditory modalities are linked with a sensory-motor approach in these Pat-a-Cake games. Rhythm is inherently important as is the rhyme. These chants also stimulate an awareness of the cadence of English rhymes.

Wolinsky (1967), while discussing the relevance of the work of Piaget to the child with learning disabilities as well as with difficulties in perception, stated, "Since the basic perceptual process develops according to this schema [the first six of Piaget's stages of intellectual development] during the sensory-motor period, any training must involve the emerging sensory-motor patterns. . . . One cannot educate for a particular defect alone, for it belies the basic integration . . . the child is groping towards" (p. 432).

The Pat-a-Cake games and chants described above link visual, auditory, and kinesthetic modalities in a sensory-motor approach. Rhythm is included, with its seemingly inherent quality of reassuring the child that he or she can come to grips with and direct the movements of his own body. At the same time, the games impart familiarity with words that rhyme.

5   Balancing and Jumping

* * * * *

The child must master the workings of his or her own body and integrate this mastery with the use of his sensory equipment and their interrelationships. This system of relationships develops during the first two years of life. The difficulties a child encounters during this period may lead to what are called learning disabilities.

In order to understand this phenomenon, we have to know what is happening in the development of children during this sensory-motor period of learning. According to Kephart (1967), children are learning specific motor patterns and skills for specific ends. A motor skill is an act produced with a high degree of precision, but is limited in scope. Motor patterns are motor skills with lesser degrees of precision and, hence, greater variability. This allows for flexibility and variation in their use. For example, a young child who has finally gotten the parts of his or her body under enough control to run, has practiced this skill and polished it to a fine degree. Let him loose in an empty room and ask him to run around the perimeter of it and he will run across the room, reach the corner, stop, make a half turn, and continue until he reaches the next corner.

The child's eyes might tend to fixate at the corner of the room as the skill is developing which would coincide with the necessity for stopping before turning the corner. Once the linking between the motor and the visual has been established, it is conceivable that the eye movements smooth out and travel around the corner, enabling the child to make the turn both physically and visually.

According to Kephart (1967), there are four motor patterns essential to the educational process that begins as soon as a child learns to stand: balance, locomotion, contact, and catching and throwing. Balance and maintenance of posture lead to the beginnings of spatial relationships through a knowledge of right and left, front and back, and up and down. Keep in mind that these notions are noncognitive in the child; they are experienced in his body. The act of locomotion, in which the child moves his or her body through space, generates information regarding the relationship between the child and objects in space. Partially seen objects can now be recognized as the whole object. The child can now keep the image of the object in his memory, and can retrieve the object even though the object may be completely hidden.

Preceding and during the development of balance and locomotion skills, contact skills are also developing. These contact activities involve manipulation, that is, reaching, grasping, and releasing. From the knowledge gained through reaching out and grasping an object, manipulating it until enough information has been gained, and then letting go, form perception, spatial relationships, and figure-ground relationships will develop.

From working with disadvantaged preschoolers, I have noted that their functioning on the Frostig perceptual tests were, for the most part, age adequate. (The Frostig is a developmental test of various forms of perception: Eye-Motor Coordination; Figure-Ground; Form Constancy; Position in Space; Spatial Relations.) Consistently lowered performance in the area of figure-ground relationships was obtained in nearly all of the children tested. Typically, these lower-class children came from large families, and, I suspect, did not receive the kind of intensive mothering more usually found in the middle-class family. I would hypothesize here that when the mothering person does not stand out prominently in the environment, the person and the background are not sharply delineated. This leads to difficulties in figure-ground discrimination.

The child with learning disabilities often has disturbances in figure-ground relationships too. When there is some distraction, this child often cannot focus attention on objects long enough to obtain enough information to understand them or to distinguish the objects adequately from their background. Or, some quality of the object may catch the child's attention so that other aspects of the object are ignored. The object is not apprehended in sufficient ways and cannot be recognized under different circumstances. On another day, the child may get different kinds of information, which also leads to confusion in attempting to conceptualize the "oneness" of the object. Thus, the child does not develop competence in gaining knowledge about the world and, therefore, in coping with the environment.

In addition to the contact skills mentioned previously, the child must learn how to place his or her body in the path of a moving object, as is necessary in catching a ball. The child must also learn how to move objects, as in throwing, hitting, pushing, and pulling. Throwing, catching, and hitting are necessary skills for many team games. Pushing and pulling are skills often used for self-protection and come into sharp focus during middle childhood. The children who have troubles in these areas are picked last for teams. They have trouble defending themselves and are often ostracized by their peers and denied important opportunities to test out and practice their abilities.

Peer rejection often implies to the child that he or she does not measure up as a girl or boy. Add to this not measuring up as a teammate and learner and we have a picture of a child who experiences himself as an incompetent. We have a vicious circle in operation.

Feelings of incompetence, unfortunately, usually begin much earlier than middle childhood, about the time that the child has to develop a system of relationships for himself. This system of relationships is based on extensive and consistent experiences. Neither of these conditions is met by the child who develops a learning disability.

The first system of relationships exists in the child's body via motor exploration. However, this is closely allied to the visual, auditory, and tactile modalities, as information is coming in through all the sense modalities concurrently. The child must match and gain the same information through motor and visual modalities for the system of relationships to grow. He must learn to explore an object with his eyes in the same way he previously explored it with his body, for it is only by moving away from sensory-motor modalities to more cognitive ones that intelligence grows and, with it, the ability to conceptualize and generalize.

Kephart (1967), in his differentiation between motor skill and motor pattern, suggests that the motor pattern is by far the more important, and is based upon the development of the skill. The first of his four basic motor patterns is balance and the maintenance of posture. All children, by the time they have developed a learning disability, have developed the skill of maintaining balance and posture, even if they seem quite clumsy.

The skill of jumping begins quite early in the development of children. Two-year-olds can be seen trying very hard to jump. However, they are afraid of lifting both feet off the ground at the same time. They will lift one foot and make believe they have jumped. They have not

accomplished the task. Approximately a year later they are more confident of their ability and can jump lifting both feet. Hopping then becomes the problem. They can stand on one foot, but lifting that foot to jump throws them into a tizzy. In time, this task, too, is mastered.

The wish to jump is seen in the child who attempts to jump rather than walk down the last step in a flight of stairs. Interest in the trampoline seems to be an extension of the desire to jump. Rope jumping also satisfies this need and requires a good deal of coordination.

Most girls try jumping with a rope at about the age of six. First, they master jumping alone and then jumping with a friend. First the skill is mastered alone, then the skill is gradually refined into a pattern so that two can do it together. Even boys may be seen jumping rope, but usually it is not because they like the game and its challenge to master a rather complicated task. They are practicing as prize fighters do, underscoring the importance of make-believe and fantasy for children.

Another way of jumping rope challenges one's skill even further. It involves jumping into a rope that two other children are turning.

As the rope game is introduced, the children must order themselves (first, second, third, and so on). Since all the children who are interested in playing cannot jump unless two are turning the rope, "enders" have to be chosen, usually designated first ender and second ender. The child who misses while jumping relieves the first ender who can join the end of the line. The second ender becomes first ender, and is relieved in the same manner. To choose enders, the rope is folded. Each child interested in playing takes a loop. All pull at the same time to open the rope. The two children who are holding the rope closest to the end become the "enders." The rest line up waiting for the turning to begin. The game proceeds very much like follow the leader. All the children usually go through the rope once to warm up and coordinate the tempos of their jumping and the rope turning. Timing of the jumping-in and jumping-out is crucial to this game. Here, too, chants are used to help. Below are some of the rhymes:

> *Room for rent*
> *Apply within*
> *When I run out*
> *You run in!*

> *　　*　　*

Strawberry shortcake cream on top
Tell me the name of your sweetheart
Is it ....? [the child jumps to each letter of the
　　alphabet until the first letter of a sweetheart's
　　name is reached; then the name is spelled]
How many babies will you have?
　　[hop until a miss]
How many rings will she get?
　　[hop until a miss]

My mother, your mother
Lives across the way
216 East Broadway
Every night they have a fight
And this is what they say:
Lady, lady, turn around [child turns around]
Lady, lady, touch the ground [touch the
    ground]
Lady, lady, show your shoe [point toe out]
Lady, lady, please skiddo [jump out of rope].

     *   *   *

Not last night but the night before
Twenty-four rabbits came knocking at my door
As I ran out they ran in
And that's the way my story begins
Spanish dancer turn around [child turns around]
Spanish dancer touch the ground [touch
    the ground]
Spanish dancer get out of town [get out of rope].

     *   *   *

Lollipop, lollipop makes me sick
Now it's time for arithmetic
One plus one equals two
Two plus two equals four
Four plus four equals eight
Now it's time for spelling
R-a-t spells rat
C-a-t spells cat
M-a-t spells mat.

     *   *   *

Fudge, fudge call the judge
Daddy's having a baby
Mommy's going crazy
Wrap it up in tissue paper
Send it down the elevator!
    [the rope is turned fast until a miss;
    the children count the floors].

     *   *   *

My mother is from England
My father is from France
My boyfriend came from the U.S.A.
With a hole in the seat of his pants!

He gave me all his peaches
He gave me all his pears
He gave me all his fifty cents
And kissed me on the stairs.

I gave him back his peaches
I gave him back his pears
I gave him back his fifty cents
And kicked him down the stairs.

*　　*　　*

I'm a little Dutch girl
Dressed in blue
And here are the things
That I can do:
Salute to the captain [salute]
Bow to the Queen [bow]
Touch the bottom
Of the submarine [touch ground].

*　　*　　*

Hello boys, do you want to flirt?
Here comes .... *in a gingham skirt*
　　[name of child jumping is inserted]
She can wiggle, she can waggle
　　[child does wiggle and waggle]
She can do the splits
　　[child pretends to do the splits]
But I'll bet you any money
She can't do this!
　　[jumper stops rope with foot].

*　　*　　*

Down in the meadows where the green grass grows
There stands ...., *as pretty as a rose*
　　[name of child]
Along came her boyfriend, and kissed her on the nose

How many kisses did she get?
[rope is turned fast till the child misses;
everyone else counts].

*   *   *

I'm a little Dutch girl
As pretty as can be
And all the boys around my block
Are crazy over me.

*   *   *

My boyfriend's name is Michael
He rides a motorcycle
With a pimple on his nose
And ten flat toes
And that's the way my story goes.

*   *   *

I had a little brother
His name was Tiny Tim
I put him in the bathtub
To teach him how to swim
He drank up all the water
Ate up all the soap
And now my baby brother
Has a belly ache.

*   *   *

Rin Tin Tin
Swallowed a pin
He went to the doctor
And the doctor wasn't in
He opened the door and fell on the floor
And that was the end of Rin Tin Tin.

*   *   *

Last night, the night before,
A lemon and a pickle came a knockin' at my door
When I went down to let them in
They hit me on the head with a rollin' pin
This is what they said to me:

Lady, lady, turn around [child turns around]
Lady, lady, touch the ground [child touches
    ground]

Lady, lady, show your shoe [child shows shoe]
Lady, lady, how old are you? [child jumps until
misses; all other children count out loud].

*   *   *

Charlie Chaplin went to France
To teach the girlies how to dance
Heel, toe, around we go [heel, toe, and
   turn around in rope]
Salute to the Captain [salute]
Bow to the Queen [bow]
Touch the bottom of the submarine
   [touch ground].

*   *   *

Sally ate a pickle
Sally ate some pie
Sally ate some sauerkraut
And thought that she would die
Whoopsie went the pickle
Whoopsie went the pie
Whoopsie went the sauerkraut
And Sally didn't die.

Some children cannot master the skill of jumping into
or getting out of the rope on time. However, they too
can be a part of the game, albeit as permanent enders. The
group of children who have mastered this complicated
form of rope jumping will have the nonjumper stand in
the middle of the rope; then they shout, "One, two, three,
jump." The enders begin turning the rope to match the
tempo of the child's jumps. In this way, a group of children may help the child who cannot jump to get the feel
of jumping in the larger rope. When lined up, children
will often cue others as to when to get into the rope. When
a child seems frightened of jumping into the turning rope,
the other children often encourage the frightened child,
too. Rope jumping for the children I have had contact
with tends to be a cooperative venture rather than competitive. For example, a group of about two dozen ten-

to twelve-year-olds announced at the beginning of summer day camp that their mothers had told them not to play with members of the opposite sex. Their leaders registered the admonitions and proceeded with a program including all the children but not requiring the boys and girls to interact with each other.

Somewhere towards the middle of the summer, halfway into the session, the group was playing on the school yard. The girls were jumping rope while the boys played Skully. After a while, the boys ceased their playing and stood about watching the jump-rope game. Finally, some of the braver boys edged over to the girls group and asked to be included in the game. It was beneath the dignity of the boys to recite the chants while they jumped, so the girls did it for them. The whole group seemed to enjoy the activity. Subsequently, the boys played Jacks and other skill games with the girls, while the girls played Skully, marbles, and baseball with the boys.

The chants described above can also be used with a rope game called Double Dutch. In this game two ropes are turned simultaneously, which calls for the jumping child to jump in double time. The enders hold a rope in either hand turning the ropes alternately toward the center. This game calls for considerable ability in both jumpers and enders.

There are other rope games which do not require the ability to jump, but are also based on Follow-the-Leader rules. In one, two children each hold one end of a rope which rests on the ground. These children gently wave the rope so that it looks like a wriggling snake. The other children jump over the rope without touching it while chanting: "R-a-t-t-l-e-s-n-a-k-e spells rattlesnake." The chanting has incorporated into it the syllabication of the word. Once the group has gone over the rope the first time, the enders wriggle the rope a little faster. The chanting remains the same throughout. With each succeeding

go-around, the rope is wriggled faster and faster, until most of the children are out.

Another rope game is High Water, Low Water. If there is a chant that goes with this one, I have forgotten it. The children you work with may be able to create their own rhymed chant for this game. Here again, enders are needed. The game begins with the rope on the ground, and the line of children step over the rope without touching it. Then the rope is raised a little higher, and then higher and higher. The leader, on the basis of skill, must decide at some point whether to jump over or to walk under the rope. If he or she jumps over the rope, the rope continues to be raised, but if he walks under the rope, it is slowly lowered. Then the children have to stoop lower and lower so as not to be touched by the rope.

A game related to balance and the maintenance of posture is the Potato-Sack Race. This is usually a team game. Here a child climbs into a potato sack, holds it up with his hands, and races with another child similarly clad across a predetermined space. The child has to traverse the space by jumping along without falling. Once he gets to the other side, he has to quickly get out of the sack, hand it to the next child on his team, and then help that child to get into the sack and start off. Teammates, meanwhile, stand around cheering their jumper on.

Another jumping game is called Cock Fight. Two children stand within a six-foot circle drawn on the floor. Each player keeps his arms folded across his chest and raises his left foot. At a signal, the "cocks" try to shove each other out of the circle. The winner of this round is challenged by another child.

Balance and jumping games are part of the repertoire of children all over the world. A game of this genre comes from the Sudan: Getting the Bride (or Groom) Home. The children choose who will be the Bride (or Groom) while the other children in the group form two teams.

One team is the protector of the Bride while the other team attacks the Bride to prevent her from reaching home. "Home" should be a designated area before the game begins. Each player, protector or attacker, must hop on one foot as he grasps the other foot behind his back with his hand. Hopping around, the team members try to protect the Bride or Groom by getting the person "home." The other team tries to prevent this from happening.

Statues is a strenuous game which draws upon a child's ability to maintain balance and keep a pose after having been pulled or twirled. All the children line up against the wall. The person who is "It" pulls, twists, or turns each child saying, "Salt, pepper, mustard, vinegar," then suddenly lets go of the child's hand. The child must stand like a statue in whatever position he lands. After each child has become a statue, "It" tells the statues what they are (for example, monsters, fairies, princesses, clown, dancer, animal). The list is long. "It" then tells the statues to come to life, and act their parts. "It" carefully watches the pantomimes and then asks the characters to become statues again. This time the children take the pose they think their character would, and "It" chooses the best pose. This child then becomes the "It."

6   Touching Activities

*   *   *   *   *

The second of the motor patterns suggested by Kephart involves contact. The characteristic of children with learning disabilities discussed by most writers in the field is the need to touch everything. Often the object is broken in the process. This grows out of the child's lack of awareness of his or her own strength. The contact motor pattern involves the skills of reaching, grasping, and letting go. This is demonstrated in the repetitive game babies play, dropping an object from their playpen or high chair, watching it fall to the ground, and then, when it is picked up, repeating this process over and over again.

According to Kephart, it is through the skills of reaching, grasping, and letting go that the child gains information about the object and begins to develop notions about relationships between objects. The longer one holds onto an object, theoretically, the greater the amount of information one gains about it. Once enough information is obtained, the child must be able to release the object, so that he can go on to the next item on his agenda. One day, I watched a fourteen-month-old baby eat Jello. He gave up using the spoon for he could neither pick the Jello up with it nor get the full spoon to his mouth. He stuffed the first few handfuls greedily into his mouth, and then something caught his attention. As he squeezed his piece of Jello, it slowly oozed through his fingers. He took another piece and repeated the process. This time he was surprised to find the Jello gone. The warmth of his hand had melted it. He repeated this process several times, and when he had satisfied his curiosity, went back to feeding himself. This is an example of but one of the myriad ways children deal with the world to obtain greater understanding of it.

Some manipulation of objects is discouraged by parents. Rather than remove those items they wish unharmed, they often tell children not to touch them. We, as parents, forget to child-proof our homes.

If our homes were completely child-proofed, we would never have to tell our children not to touch. This is an impossibility. Nevertheless, by putting as much away as possible, the likelihood of our saying "Don't touch" will be lessened. First we encourage the contact, then unreasonably discourage it. Holding our infants, cuddling them, comforting them when they are hurt by holding them encourage the desire for contact. I am not suggesting that we do away with this, for no child develops adequately or normally without this cuddling, as the studies Harry Harlow (1959) did with baby monkeys point out. A note in the February 1976 issue of *Psychology Today* stated that stroking, cuddling, and handling of premature babies enables their nervous systems to develop more rapidly than in premature babies who did not receive this treatment. While a full-term infant may not need as much physical contact as does the premature infant, this finding suggests that all infants must have handling for physical maturation. Young children through second grade seek out physical contact with an adult in the environment, even if the child only leans against the adult and there is no reciprocity. The need for contact may be one motive of children coming up to the teacher's desk for information; it may look as if the child is trying to avoid his or her seat work.

The junior high school student will tolerate an adult touching him or her. If the student is intense about an issue, a touch may have a calming influence. However, an adolescent in high school usually resents any physical contact with an adult. The socialization process, with its admonition of "don't touch," has begun to have its impact. Nevertheless, high school students may look for, provoke, and enjoy wrestling with adults. Touching objects and people is hard to give up. We encourage lack of contact too soon. Children seem to need contact for longer periods than we have been willing to allow.

One of the remediation techniques used with children with learning disabilities is to put some objects into a paper bag, have the children close their eyes, then put their hands inside the bag and feel for an object, describe it, and tell everyone what the object is. While this is a good idea for children with learning problems, it does not go far enough. Relationships between the objects are not defined, and without these relationships, the knowledge remains fragmented. Generalizations lead to concepts, and without conceptualizations, children do not learn properly. One way of encouraging the development of the perception of relationships between objects is to use the technique described above, but have the child describe each object and help him to create a story about it. Start with a small group. Have one child describe one of the objects in the bag; then have all the children work cooperatively on the story. For example, the first child describes an object and begins the story; the next child describes an object and adds to the story; the third child describes another object and tells another piece of the story; and this continues until all the children in the group have added to the story. A group of five children works best for this type of activity. Each object can be in its own bag, and each child can have his or her own bag.

If there are errors in tactile perception, the children

can still create stories on the basis of their faulty perceptions. The objects can then be taken out of the bags for the children to look at and then create new stories based on their visual recognition of the object. The group would still take part in the creation of the new story.

Discussions may be conducted on why there are different stories based on the different perceptions and how knowing what an object is, rather than just guessing, contributed to more accurate storytelling. Concentration is also encouraged, for each child must listen to the descriptions in order to develop a comprehensible story. Each group could have the same objects but, in the long run, develop different stories. Discussions about why they are different develop the notion that different people can experience the same things in different ways, which are neither right nor wrong, a lesson many of us have forgotten in the course of living in a rather complicated world.

Collages can be made using different kinds of tactile material. Ask the children to create their own pictures (which do not have to be representational) using specific tactile experiences. For instance, they can be asked to make something that has a furry quality, combined with a rough texture and a smooth texture. Materials that possess these qualities could be available in a box. Later, the children might be asked to create these textures using paints and crayons. Thus they are encouraged first to demonstrate complete understanding of contact sensations with the materials and then to move to the next level of development, creating these sensations through the visual modality.

The materials of the plastic arts, such as clay, paper mache, and finger paint, provide the child with contact sensations, especially if experimentation with the material is allowed (for example, making the material too soft to deal with or too hard to handle). Making dough, using

fingers to mix rather than an implement, also provides
contact sensations. Making "play-dough" rather than buy-
ing it, using fingers to mix, again provides the touching
children look for. Play-dough can be made using equal
parts of flour and table salt and adding water colored with
food coloring. As one works with this mixture, it becomes
less grainy. While using these materials, the children
should discuss the sensations the materials impart to an-
chor the tactile experience with cognitive and visual experiences. Finger paints can also be made. Use equal parts
of Ivory flakes and powdered starch, and add water-base
paints for the coloring. Shelving paper or a table top can
be used in place of regular finger paint paper, which makes
this activity beneficial not only to the child, but also to
the pocketbook. While touching activities are usually
construed as feeling an object, they can also include
touching or being aware of various parts of the body.
Below is a chant and activity to help children become
aware of their hands, head, feet, and arms.

> *If I move one finger* [right hand in fist,
>   free forefinger and wiggle]
> *And wiggle my thumb* [keep fist,
>   wiggle right thumb]
> *I have two fingers moving* [right thumb and
>   forefinger wiggle]
> *By gum!* [clap hands twice to rhythm of words]
> *By gum!* [nod twice]
>
> *If I move two fingers* [wiggle both forefingers,
>   rest of hand in fist]
> *And wiggle both thumbs* [wiggle both thumbs]
> *I have four fingers moving* [wiggle both
>   forefingers and both thumbs]
> *By gum!* [clap twice]
> *By gum!* [nod twice]
>
> *If I move four fingers* [wiggle four fingers
>   of right hand]

And wiggle my thumb [wiggle right thumb]
I have five fingers moving [wiggle all five
    fingers of right hand]
By gum! [clap twice]
By gum! [nod twice]

If I move eight fingers [wiggle four fingers
    on each hand]
And wiggle both thumbs [wiggle both thumbs]
I have ten fingers moving [wiggle all fingers
    of both hands]
By gum! [clap twice]
By gum! [nod twice]

If I move both arms [move both arms,
    hands in fists]
And I wiggle my thumbs [wiggle both thumbs]
I have arms and thumbs moving [move both
    arms and wiggle thumbs]
By gum! [clap twice]
By gum! [nod twice]

If I move both feet [shuffle both feet]
And wiggle my thumbs [wiggle both thumbs]
I have feet and thumbs moving [move feet
    and wiggle thumbs at same time]
By gum! [clap twice]
By gum! [nod twice]

If I stand and sit [stand up, sit down]
And wiggle my thumbs [wiggle both thumbs]
I'll get awful tired [no motion]
And I'll quit; By gum! [two big claps]

Another touching game is This Is My Elbow. The children should be seated in a circle, for greater visibility, while one child, who is "It" stands in the middle. He or she holds one ear and says, "This is my elbow," and names one child in the circle. The named child must then hold his or her elbow and say "This is my ear" before

"It" counts to five, or he becomes the new "It." If the wrong part is held, the child becomes the new "It." If the child can accomplish this task, "It" goes on to holding his chin, stating "This is my nose," and calling upon another child. Any number of variations is possible using different body parts.

7 Catching and Throwing Games

* * * * *

The last of the motor patterns discussed by Kephart involves objects in space and the process of stopping movement and imparting movement to objects. These are called receipt and propulsion patterns. They can be seen in the child's ability to sight and catch a ball and to throw it accurately so that someone else can catch it. The passivity that characterizes many children leaves little room for the development of these skills. I realize that many children take part in Little League ball games. However, great skill is needed to play these games, which have been forced upon children. The skills were not developed from necessity or simply because a child has practiced for mastery because he enjoys it.

The motor skills involved in receipt and propulsion patterns require learning about one's body, knowing what it can do, what it cannot do, and how to use it as efficiently as is possible. Some delightful games can be used to help children to focus in on what it feels like to wiggle various parts of their bodies.

Here We Go, Looby Loo, which depends upon the use of body parts, can be used with a discussion about what it feels like to shake various parts of the body. Talk about

how the hand, arm, foot, leg, head, and so on, felt as they were shaken.

The children form a circle; while walking around, alternately move to the right and then the left, chanting:

Here we go, Looby Loo
Here we go, Looby La
Here we go, Looby Loo
All on a Saturday night.

I put my right hand in
I take my right hand out
I give my right hand a shake, shake, shake
And turn myself about.

Chorus: Here we go, Looby Loo, etc.

I put my left hand in
I take my left hand out
I give my left hand a shake, shake, shake
And turn myself about.

Chorus

I put my right foot in
I take my right foot out
I give my right foot a shake, shake, shake
And turn myself about.

Chorus

I put my left foot in
I take my left foot out
I give my left foot a shake, shake, shake
And turn myself about.

Chorus

I put my right arm in
I take my right arm out
I give my right arm a shake, shake, shake
And turn myself about.

Chorus

I put my left arm in
I take my left arm out
I give my left arm a shake, shake, shake
And turn myself about.

Chorus

I put my right leg in
I take my right leg out
I give my right leg a shake, shake, shake
And turn myself about.

Chorus

I put my left leg in
I take my left leg out
I give my left leg a shake, shake, shake
And turn myself about.

Chorus

I put my whole head in
I take my whole head out
I give my head a shake, shake, shake
And turn myself about.

Chorus

I put my whole self in
I take my whole self out
I give my whole self a shake, shake, shake
And turn myself about.

Chorus

Simon Says is another game that gives a child a better sense of body parts. The children follow what the leader directs as long as he or she says "Simon says" first. If the leader states "Put your hands up" without first saying "Simon says," the children should not do anything. Touching body parts, crossing the midline, and crossing arms and touching knees, shoulders, or elbows are examples of directions.

Copying the motions of another child helps a child learn and understand the parts of the body. The ability to copy can be accomplished through fun activities. One of the games uses a circle; it involves singing a song and keeping time to the music and following the movements of a leader. One child goes into the middle of the circle while the other children sing:

> *Did you ever see a lassie* [or laddie,
>   depending upon the sex of the child
>   in center]
> *A lassie, a lassie*
> *Did you ever see a lassie*
> *Go this way and that*
> *Go this way and that way*
> *Go this way and that way*
> *Did you ever see a lassie*
> *Go this way and that?*

During the singing, the child in the center performs movements both to the right and to the left of his or her body. The children of the circle imitate the child in the center after the first demonstration. Then the child in the center chooses another child to go into the center and create another movement.

Some circle games have no particular emphasis on directionality, but rather on bodily movement and control over one's body. In this one, a child stands in the center of the circle. The rest chant:

> *We are going to Kentucky*
> *We are going to the fair*
> *To see the senorita*
> *With the flowers in her hair*
> *Oh shake it, shake it, shake it*
> *And do the best you can*
> *Rumble to the bottom*
> *Rumble to the top*
> *Turn around, and turn around*
> *Until you make a stop.*

The children move around the circle holding hands, singing the chant until the line: "To see the senorita," at which point one child goes into the center. On "Oh shake," the child begins to shake his body as if he were doing the twist. On "Rumble to the bottom," the child shakes his body as he begins to squat and then slowly stands up again as he continues to shake his body. The child then turns around quickly, with his eyes closed, and stops on the word "stop," pointing his finger at the child facing him, who then becomes the next to enter the circle.

Pantomime is another activity that is based upon knowledge of one's body in space. With the following game, word families can be incorporated in the activity.

The group is divided into two teams. Team One decides upon a word (for example, hand). The captain of team One tells team Two that the word rhymes with "stand." Team Two then pantomimes a word that rhymes. Team One must decipher the word and state "No it is not a band." Team Two then tries again. When the team figures out the word, it chooses the next word for team One to decipher.

Another pantomime game involves the acting out of a broken-down car. This activity calls for a group of six children who choose the name of an automobile. Each player then acts out one aspect of disrepair for example:

> Number 1—steering gear is broken—
>   walk zig-zag
> Number 2—flat tire—limp
> Number 3—water in the gas—
>   two steps forward, one step back
> Number 4—can't go forward—walk backward
> Number 5—can't go at all
> Number 6—push number 5 by placing both
>   hands on player's waist

The team performing all acts correctly in the shortest time wins. This is done standing in a line.

We have, in these circle games, the beginnings of receipt and propulsion skills via the use of the child's own body. Once they have been mastered to some degree one can proceed to help the children develop these skills as applied to objects in space.

The plethora of children's games that have as a basis receipt and propulsion skills, suggests that these skills are the most difficult to master and that they need the most practice. At first, practice takes place at the most basic level, where the child puts his own body into motion, stopping the motion at will. From there, the child moves on to putting other objects into motion in a variety of ways. And he learns how to stop objects in a variety of ways.

If we begin with the use of balls, all sorts of games quickly come to mind: Baseball, Running Bases, Monkey-in-the-Middle, Dodge Ball, and Kickball. However, there are games using balls that call for greater and greater refinement of skill with imparting propulsion to the ball that have long disappeared; these also require a number of other skills.

Bouncing a ball is the basis for the next series of games. This requires a sense of timing, ability to catch quickly and continue to bounce, knowledge of the alphabet, ability to tell stories, and some knowledge of geography.

The child bounces the ball while telling this story:

> *A, my name is Anna* [or any other girl's name
>   beginning with A]
> *And my husband's name is Al* [or any other boy's
>   name beginning with A]
> *We come from Alabama* [or any other place with
>   the beginning letter of A]
> *And we sell Apples* [or anything else salable
>   beginning with A].

Each letter of the alphabet is used in a similar manner. The object of this game is to continuously bounce the

ball without missing while turning one leg over the ball and continuing the story, first on the A's, then B's, then C's, and so on through the alphabet. A great deal of co-ordination is required to keep the ball going, to remember the story line, to remember to put one leg over the ball on the right letter, and then to get through the alphabet. When a child misses, he or she picks up on the letter missed on the next turn rather than beginning from A each time.

A more complicated version of this game involves the development of a story line in accordance with one's ability to turn one leg over the ball a number of times in succession. In this game, the story must be completed within a short time, but cannot be a one or two liner. The children, at the start of the game, may decide on a minimum number of leg turns for the story. This game pulls upon the child's ability to tell a story coherently, for a child is out if he forgets to put his leg over the ball, cannot finish the story, or tells a story that is not coherent. Here are some examples.

> In America Armanda and her husband Armond took a trip to Atlanta to see the ant hills. In Atlanta they arrived at the ant hill but the ants did not come out of the hill to greet them when they arrived. So Armanda and her husband Armond left the ant hill and Atlanta and went back home to Australia.

> Betty Boop bought bananas for her boyfriend, but her boyfriend Bobby did not like bananas. So Betty Boop took the bananas that her boyfriend Bobby did not like to her brother Bernie.

The children can make up any story as long as it has a goodly number of words beginning with the letter they are supposed to use and the story is complete. Stories become more complicated as the children become more pro-

ficient in the game. In this way, they can show off their
prowess in handling the ball and in their ability to tell a
long, complicated story using words beginning with the
same letter.

Another bouncing-ball game involves the use of geography. This game must be completed from A to Z in one
turn, or the child must begin again from the beginning.
Again, the child must turn his or her leg over the ball
on each succeeding letter of the alphabet. This ball game
begins "I took a trip around the world and this is where
I went. From America to Boston, from Boston to Colorado, from Colorado to Denmark, from Denmark to
England," and so on through the alphabet.

With the ball games described above, skills in receipt
and propulsion are developed along with storytelling skills,
use of alphabet knowledge, balance skills, and geography
knowledge.

Hopscotch, or Potsy, is a game that uses receipt and
propulsion skills in addition to balance patterns. Each
child should find his or her own stone or counter which
he uses to throw onto a number without touching the
lines of the box (see diagram 1).

First the child throws a marker onto the square marked
1, hops into the box marked 2, hops into 3, hops onto 4
and 5 (one foot in each box), hops into 6, hops onto 7
and 8. He then turns his body around in the 7 and 8 box,
hops back into 6, hops into 4 and 5, hops into 3, hops
into 2, and then leans over and picks up the marker in 1
while standing on one foot, then hops out. He continues
his turn, tossing the marker into square 2 on the next
throw. Throughout all of these maneuvers, if the child
steps on a line, or his marker falls on a line, he is out.
On his next turn the child begins where he last went out.
He does not have to begin from the beginning each time.
Once the child has completed all eight numbers, he starts
with 8 and goes back toward 1. When he has completed

Diagram 1: Hopscotch

the game both ways, he stands with his back to the boxes and throws his marker onto a square. If it lands within a square, the child marks it off as his own, which means that the other children cannot step into this box, but must jump over it.

An alternate form of Hopscotch is to gently kick the marker from one number to another without stepping on the line and without the marker landing on the line or out of bounds. The child, once he has kicked the marker through the boxes successfully, will then choose a second marker, which he carries on the back of his hand, on his forehead, or on his shoulder.

Then there is Category Hopscotch. This game needs a forty-five inch square marked off into nine fifteen-inch squares. Before the game proceeds, a category is decided upon. The child must hop on one foot in each box, and, in even rhythm, name an item in the category. The same foot is used throughout the nine squares. Each time there is a miss, the child begins again. Categories could include:

1. Countries
2. Wild animals
3. Rhyming words
4. Multiplication tables
5. Word families
6. Presidents
7. States
8. Colors

There is also an English form of Hopscotch which uses a two-footed jump with the marker held between the feet. The object of the game is to jump through all six boxes (a thirty by forty-five inch area is marked off into six fifteen-inch squares numbered from one to six), without dropping the stone or stepping on a line. This game could also be used for the development of balance and jumping skills.

Jumpscotch is a game using a forty-five-inch square divided into nine fifteen-inch boxes. The four sides of the large square are numbered sequentially. As you face side one, the row of three boxes nearest to you is marked A, 1, B; the second row, C, 2, D; the third row, E, 3, F. The object of this game is to get the right sequencing. After you become acquainted with this game, other markings can be used to teach whatever concepts are necessary for the children. The child jumps, using both feet, into the center square of side one, and then jumps, putting one foot into each of the other squares, then back into one with both feet, and then out backwards. Then the child jumps over 1 into 2 with both feet, then into C and D, back into 2, then into 1, then out. Then the child jumps over 1 and 2 into 3, then into E and F, back into 3, into 2, into 1, and then out. When this sequence is completed without stepping on a line, without starting on the wrong square, or without mixing up the sequence, the child goes through the same sequence on side two, then three, then four. As the children become proficient with this sequence, new sequences can be devised. The children can work in a team or with partners, depending on what seems necessary for their growth.

In Snail Hopscotch (see diagram 1), the child tosses a marker into square 1, hops in, and with careful control, kicks the marker into squares 2, 3, 4, and so on, without stepping on a line, and without the marker landing on a line or out of bounds. The child must hop on the same foot until he or she reaches the rest area and can stand on both feet. The child must then hop the marker back through the squares. If the child goes through successfully, he may choose a square, which can be used as an additional resting place by that child on the next round. All the other children must hop their markers over the square and may not hop into it. If the child misses, he must begin at 1 again. If the child misses coming back from rest, he can begin at rest; he does not have to begin at 1.

The use of six sidewalk-size squares (about four feet by four feet) is important for the following game (see diagram 2). A child rolls a ball into the first box, hops in after it, bounces it once, skips into the next box with one foot, bounces the ball once, and so on, around the six boxes. With this game the child must develop great skill so that the ball is rolled into the sixth box from square number 1 slowly enough for him to skip through the five other boxes, reaching the sixth box before the ball rolls over the line. In both Hopscotch and this form of Box Ball, the child must not only consider how to throw a marker or roll a ball, but also must be able to maintain balance while jumping and skipping, and at the same time pay attention to where he is putting his feet so as to avoid the lines which will make him lose his turn.

A game of greater skill using receipt and propulsion patterns is called Skully. In this game children collect bottle caps. In years past, they melted crayons and filled the caps so that each child knew which cap belonged to him. The markers are placed in the home space, moving out from there through twelve numbers and then home again. As the children move their markers through the twelve numbers, they try to knock their opponents' markers off the numbers. The caps are moved by a flick of the middle finger against the thumb. With this game, not only receipt and propulsion skills are used, but eye-hand coordination as well.

Marble shooting draws upon the same series of skills. Here, holes large enough to accommodate a marble easily are made in a cigar box (diagram 3). The object of this game is to shoot a marble through one of the holes in the box. If the marble goes through, the child earns a predetermined number of marbles. If the marble does not

Diagram 2: Boxes

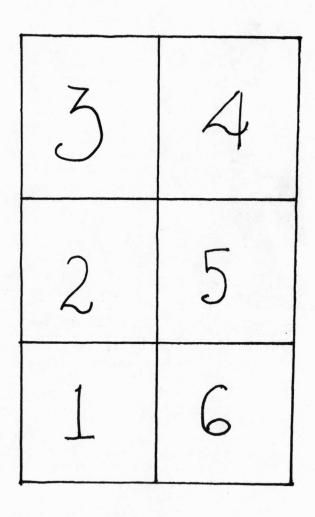

go through one of the holes, the child who owns the
cigar box collects the errant marble.

The same cigar box can be used for another marble
game. The box is backed against a step or curve with the
cover down, creating a ramp (see diagram 3). The
players stand at a predetermined distance from the box
and try to roll their marbles into the box. While this seems
like a relatively easy game to win, the problem entails
learning how much speed must be used to reach the target.
Too slow and the marble does not make it up the ramp;
too fast and the marble hits the sides of the box and re-
bounds out. The halfway mark between shooting line and
ramp is marked. If the marble rolls back over this halfway
mark, the shooter can use the marble again. If not, the
owner of the box keeps the marble. The sharp-shooter
who gets a marble into the box gets a five to one (or
some other predetermined odds) return on his marble.

When I was a child, these two marble games were favorites of the neighborhood, and heralded the beginning
of autumn. At that time, the children would stop at the
candy store around the corner (in those days all the stores
were around the corner), ask the owner for a drink of
water, casually glance at the cigar case, and then ask for
an empty cigar box. If you were one of the early ones,
there was usually a cigar box available. When you waited
too long you had to come back tomorrow or next week.
There were many games going at one time.

Another favorite box for games was the wooden kind
that cream cheese came in. Children would wait around
in the grocery store until the cream cheese was all sold
so as to be the first to request that hard-to-come-by wooden
box. A hole was made in the bottom of this box, some-
what larger than the largest marble in use that year. A
child would stand straddling the box with its bottom
side up and try to drop a marble into the hole. The owner
of the box kept the marbles that did not drop through the

Diagram 3: Marbles

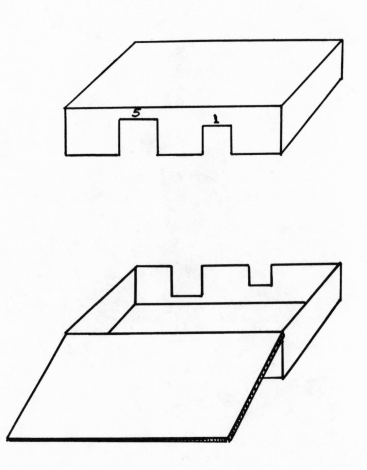

hole. Since this was a hard game to win, the winners usually got about a ten-to-one return on their marbles.

Jacks is another game in this series. This game is usually played by girls but intrigues boys as well and requires a great deal of skill in throwing a ball, catching, and other eye-hand coordinations. A school in our district has a Jack-playing contest each spring, which gives the children time to practice and perfect their skills during the rest of the school year.

Ten jacks are held in one hand; a small ball rests on top of the fist covering the jacks. The ball is thrown in the air and the jacks are placed on the floor. The ball is caught by the same hand after one bounce. Then the ball is thrown in the air and the child picks up one jack. The ball is caught with the same hand after the first bounce. This procedure is used for picking up each of the ten jacks. The whole group of jacks is again held in the hand and put down as described before, but on this round two jacks are picked up each time, then three, then four, and so on. As in Pick Up Sticks, you may not touch a jack you are not picking up.

Pick Up Sticks can be found in at least two sizes: small, slim sticks for the older children and long, fat sticks for the younger child. In this game, eye-hand coordination can be practiced, and a child can learn to impart movement to only one stick at a time. Directions for playing come with the game.

8 Games and Ages

* * * * *

In the previous chapters we have discussed games in terms of sense modalities and motor patterns, without consideration of the age level or emotional needs of the child.

Four-Year-Olds

Children of four enjoy physical activity using the large muscles. Hopping and skipping are usually beyond their abilities. Jumping, climbing, and running, which use large muscles, are the favored activities. Interest in balance activities, such as walking on ledges, cracks, and the curb, are indications of a trend towards finer control over the use of the large muscles, which will eventually be transferred to use of the smaller muscles of the hands. In conjunction with use of the small muscles of the hand is a growing interest in painting, coloring, finger painting, and doing play-dough and clay work, all activities which enable fine motor coordination to be practiced.

Four-year-olds are imaginative and curious. They tend to ask endless why questions, some of which are directed toward adults in the environment. Others the child tries to answer for him/herself through the medium of socio-dramatic play. At this age, imaginative play, imitation,

and pantomime are at their height. Games, songs, and rhythms (where a child interprets music and then acts out the feelings it evokes) are good activities to include in a program for children of this age. Here are two panto-mime activities appropriate for this age level.

I have ten little fingers; [extend fingers]
They all belong to me; [point to self]
I can make them do things;
Would you like to see?

I can open them up wide; [spread fingers apart]
Shut them up tight; [make fists]
Put them together; [touch palms together]
Put them out of sight; [put hands behind back]
Jump them up high; [raise hands]
Jump them down low; [lower hands to floor]
Fold them quietly and sit just so. [fold in lap]

  *   *   *

Open, shut them
Open, shut them [open fingers wide; then make fist]
Give a little clap [clap hands]

Open, shut them
Open, shut them [open fingers wide, make fist]
Lay them in your lap [hands in lap]

Creep them, creep them
Creep them, creep them [slowly creep fingers up body]

Right up to your chin
Open your little mouth [open mouth]
But do not put them in

Open, shut them
Open, shut them [open hands wide; then make a fist]
To your shoulders fly ["fly" hands to shoulders]

Then like little birds
Let them flutter to the sky [flutter fingers up—
      "fly" them]
Falling, falling, falling
Almost to the ground [fly fingers down]

Quickly pick them up again [hold hands in the air]
And turn them round and round [twist hands
      back and forth]
Faster, faster, faster, faster [move hands fast]
Slower, slower, slower, slower [move hands slow]
Clap [clap hands]

FIVE-YEAR-OLDS

The five-year-old, compared to the four-year-old, is more controlled and less daring. Whereas the four-year-old did not like to comply with adult demands and expectations, the five-year-old is quite compliant. By now, the child can skip, hop, and maintain balance on one leg. Since the child is no longer as daring as he was at four, he prefers to do not only those things that are familiar, but also those things that he can do well. Routine seems to be the byword at this age.

Skipping games, kick ball, and simple rope games are well within the ability of the five-year-old. Dramatic singing games, such as Here We Go Round the Mulberry Bush, Sing a Song of Six Pence, or Blue Bird, are favorites.

Fine motor coordination is greatly improved so that lacing shoes and buttoning buttons are accomplished with greater dexterity. Cutting and pasting activities such as collage making are enjoyed by the five-year-old. Sociodramatic play, while not as intense at five as it was at four, is still an important activity.

In the Railroad Train game, each child takes the part of some object on or a part of a train: conductor; cowcatcher; caboose; engine; coal car; wheels; whistle; bell; and so on. An adult plays the role of the station master and tells a story. He might say, "We must hurry and make up a train leaving for Colorado. We need a caboose, an engine, a coal car, and a whistle." The children line up single file behind the starter as they are named. All the parts need to be "hooked together" before the train can start. Then the starter pulls out of the station, goes through a tunnel, over a bridge, around a curve, up a mountain, down a hill, and any other activities a train might do before pulling into the next station.

A circle game appropriate for five-year-olds is Charlie Over the Water. The children alternately circle right and left singing or saying:

> *Charlie over the water,*
> *Charlie over the sea,*
> *Charlie catch a blackbird,*
> *But can't catch me.*

A "Charlie" is chosen at the beginning and stands in the middle of the circle watching the players carefully. As the rhyme is completed, all the children stoop to avoid being tagged by Charlie. A tagged player becomes the new Charlie.

SIX-YEAR-OLDS

The six-year-old is like the four-year-old. He has boundless energy that takes him into all kinds of situations, some dangerous. Being first, winner, or best is of crucial importance. In make-believe play, the six-year-old *becomes* the character he is playing, rather than "just pretending" as he did at four and five. Once again the child is resistive to adult directions and demands, wanting his own way. Nevertheless, the six-year-old is quite vulnerable; his feelings are easily hurt, especially when criticized or corrected. With his high levels of energy and propensities for running, jumping, and climbing, some rather strenuous activities and games are in order. Keep in mind, however, that a child of this age, while able to function well in a group, cannot do so for long periods of time. Relay or team games should be interspersed with individual-oriented games such as Jack Be Nimble. In this game, the children line up to await their turn jumping over an object about six to nine inches in height. As the child jumps, the rest of the group sings:

> *Jack be nimble,*
> *Jack be quick.*
> *Jack jump over*
> *The candlestick.*

Circle games, such as Dodge Ball, are good for this age group. The child is more coordinated and can now catch and throw a ball with greater accuracy. One must keep in mind, however, that when a six-year-old throws a ball, he or she will throw it as hard and as far as his skill will allow.

Six-year-olds, like four- and five-year-olds, enjoy miming and action games. Here is one using concepts of right and left.

> *This is my right hand, raise it up high*
> [raise right hand]
> *This is my left hand, I'll touch the sky*
> [reach for sky]
> *Right hand, left hand, whirl them around*
> [circle hands in front of body]
> *Left hand, right hand, pound, pound, pound.*
> [pound left and right fists together]
>
> *This is my right foot, tap, tap, tap*

> [tap right foot three times]
> *This is my left foot, tap, tap, tap*
> [tap left foot three times]
> *Right foot, left foot, run, run, run*
> [run in place]
> *Right foot, left foot, jump for fun.*
> [jump in place]
>
> *Up to the ceiling, down to the floor*
> [raise both hands high; lower them to floor]
> *Right to the windows, left to the door.*
> [move both hands right and left]
>
> *My right hand I raise* [follow action]
> *My right hand I shake*
> *Around my head a circle make.*
>
> *I bow to the left* [follow action]
> *I bow to the right*
> *And I turn around with footsteps so light.*

Poor Pussy is a game that has appeal for the six-year-old. The children sit in a circle. One child is chosen to be the pussy. Pussy kneels in front of a child and meows. The child pats pussy three times, saying each time, "Poor pussy." In the meantime, pussy tries to make the child smile. If pussy accomplishes this goal pussy and the child exchange places. If not, pussy tries to make another child smile.

Crossing the Brook is a rather simple game involving broad jumping. A running commentary describing the child's behavior adds interest and appeal for the six-year-old, who still likes to make believe. A brook can be marked off on the ground, about twenty-four inches wide. This distance can be increased as the children gain proficiency in jumping. Stones in the water can be represented by markers. These stones can be used to jump on in place of jumping clear across the brook. Children line up to take turns crossing the brook. If a child doesn't make it, comments such as "Jane fell in the water," "She's all wet,"

"She can't get back to the stone," "Now she has to wade across the brook," "It's getting deeper and deeper," "It's up to her waist," "Ah! She's gotten across; now she has to take off those wet shoes and socks," add enjoyment for the six-year-old.

SEVEN-YEAR-OLDS

Seven-year-olds, by contrast with six-year-olds, are subdued, almost depressed. As they are calmer physically than they have been before, they tend to stick with an activity for longer periods of time. Their approach to tasks leads an observer to conclude that they are making serious attempts to develop skills and competencies. While they are more interested in people as well as more sensitive to and aware of the attitudes of others, there are still frequent squabbles with peers.

Physical maturation has taken a great leap forward in the year from six to seven. The seven-year-old loves to play baseball and other games that depend upon and help develop eye-hand coordination. Marble games as well as hopscotch games are activities that readily engage the imagination of the seven-year-old. Skully and Here We Go Looby Loo are also appropriate activities.

EIGHT-YEAR-OLDS

Eight-year-olds are outgoing and exhibit keen interest in adults and adult activities. They often hang around, usually when they are least welcome, and listen to adult conversations. Along with this development is the beginning of hero worship and imitation and emulation of the idol. Baseball cards become a major interest. Eight-year-olds are eager for new experiences. With their high energy levels, active games with simple rules, such as the various forms of tag, hide and seek, rope jumping, and dodge ball, are just right. Children of this age are also exaggerators and dramatizers who can chew your ear off with their seemingly endless verbalizations. Short plays and other forms of dramatization in songs and games are welcome by this noisy age group.

NINE-YEAR-OLDS

Nine is a difficult age. To paraphrase Fritz Redl (1966), it is the time when the nicest children behave in the awfullest manner. It is not surprising, then, that more children of this age are referred to mental health clinics than children of other ages. Nine-year-olds tend to be moody, complaining, lacking in self-confidence, self-depreciating, unable to make decisions, and very critical of others. However, what concerns adults most is the nine-year-olds' apparent loss of important social skills. Children drop their clothes anywhere, refuse to bathe, can't seem to sit still, develop tics and odd body postures, and sometimes begin wetting their beds at night. A conversation with a nine-year-old often deals with gory and unusual events. Adults need to be reassured that this is a passing phase. These symptoms are a prelude to adolescence.

On the positive side, the nine-year-old works hard to develop specific skills not only for him- or herself but also to enhance group functioning. The use of games, therefore, needs to address the nine-year-old's interest in developing individual skills and his or her need to use these skills for team and group games and sports. Part of the motivation for developing skills is to test one's abilities against the abilities of same-sex peers. Girls usually prefer to play with girls, and boys with boys. The games described in previous chapters are most appropriate for nine-, ten-, and eleven-year-olds, while individual skills can be developed through gymnastics and stunts.

TEN THROUGH TWELVE

Children of ages ten through twelve are similar in interest level, motor skills, and abilities. However, they do differ in personality. Ten-year-olds are rather straightforward, matter-of-fact people, who seem relatively at ease with themselves and the world. They are more accepting of adult-imposed structure than they were at nine and, hence, seem docile and agreeable by comparison. Eleven-year-olds, on the other hand, are antagonistic and contrary. But, they are responsive to people in spite of being quarrelsome and critical.

Eleven-year-olds are quite verbal and tend to go on in endless detail, which may be a response to an inability to make decisions. By the time the eleven-year-old reaches twelve, it is apparent that a toning-down process has taken place. While twelve-year-olds are energetic, enthusiastic, and ready for new experiences, they are also more responsive to the environment. A twelve-year-old tends to conform and become an integral part of the peer group.

Preference for group life is the umbrella characteristic of the ten- to twelve-year-old age group. During this period of their lives, children exhibit great loyalty to their peer group. A team game is deemed so important that they will resist the rules and regulations of home to continue the game. In conjunction with this characteristic is the child's drive to develop the skills the group needs most to win. Ten- to twelve-year-olds are quite competitive and work hard to win, either for themselves or their group. Volleyball, football, baseball, basketball, and soccer are some of the competitive team games appropriate for this age level.

Thus far we have discussed developmental themes which one could be expected to observe in typical children. The learning disabled child is quite often out of developmental phase with his peers. When we observe the behaviors of this type of child, since they seem to be different from others of the same age, we too often conclude that these behaviors are abnormal. In his Nobel Prize acceptance address, Tinbergen, a behavioral scientist, made a comment that reminded me of an important fact that I had long forgotten. If we could divorce ourselves from the notion of "abnormal," we would be free to understand that the behaviors we see, while perhaps inappropriate for the current age of a child, may be appropriate at some earlier period of development. However, a nine-year-old who exhibits the behaviors and concerns of a four-year-old cannot be treated as a four-year-old. This child is not really like a four-year-old, as he has had an additional four or five years of living. Helping the child deal with the four-year-old's concerns while respecting and treating the nine-year-old self is a difficult job. Games, stories, stunts, make-believe, and pantomime are some of the vehicles by which an adult can help the child to grow emotionally so that he can catch up with his physical and chronological development. A game level should be matched with the physical and cognitive ability of the child, while the content level of the game should address the emotional needs.

A game from Tanzania called My Children Come to Me could be helpful to children who have had difficulty making an identification with an appropriate role model. Alternating the role the child plays in this game may enable the child to make the identification. One player is Mother Hen or Father Rooster and another is the Hawk. The rest of the children are the flock of chicks. Two lines about sixty feet apart are drawn on the ground. The Hen or Rooster stands behind one line, the Chicks stand behind the other, and the Hawk roams in between. The dialogue, repeated twice, begins the game:

> Hen (or Rooster): *My children, come to me.*
> Chicks: *We can't.*
> Hen (or Rooster): *Why not?*
> Chicks: *Because the hawk is near.*

The Hen or Rooster calls a third time and the Chicks try

to run across the area safely without being caught by the Hawk. Those Chicks tagged by the Hawk become little Hawks during the next round of the game. Other games described throughout the book can be adapted for special needs of children.

9   Word Games

* * * * *

While the chants associated with the games described in these chapters introduce children to rhythm, rhyming, and the cadence of the language, they also provide children with the opportunity to play with words and ideas. The choosing chant:

> *Intery, mintery, cutery, corn*
> *Apple seed and apple thorn*
> *Wire, briar, limber lock*
> *How many geese to make a flock?*
> *One flew east and one flew west*
> *One flew over the cuckoo's nest*

does not make sense, but it does provide a child with an opportunity to play with words. The chant:

> *Dickery, dickery, dare*
> *The pig flew up in the air*
> *The man in brown*
> *Soon brought him down*
> *Dickery, dickery, dare.*

provides the child with the opportunity to say what is not true. If you ask a child of five or six to state that coal is white or snow is black he would probably balk. Children are aware of an object's color and will argue about it, but they cannot verbalize the apparent contradiction. This chant, if used a few years later, is accepted by the child. He is not bothered by the idea of a pig flying when he knows it cannot do so in reality. In a sense, the children are saying that they can override the reality of the situation for a while in favor of the rules of the chant. A game that embodies this notion is This Is My Nose, which begins with all the children sitting in a circle. One child is chosen "It" and stands before a seated child. "It" places a hand on some part of his own body, for example, his nose, and says "This is my elbow." The player addressed must grasp his elbow and say "This is my nose" before "It" counts to ten. If he fails, he becomes "It."

Another game that involves playing with words is Prince of Paris. The players sit in a circle, except the one who has been chosen as the leader. The players (P) number themselves off. The leader (L) says: "The Prince of Paris has lost his hat. Did you find it number ....?"

P: Who, sir? I, sir?
L: Yes sir, you sir.
P: No sir, not I sir.
L: Then who sir?
P: Number .... sir.

The person whose number is called starts the dialogue again saying: "Who sir? I sir?" Any mistake causes the erring player to go to the end of the numbering system, moving the others up one number. In this game the children not only must be alert to their numbers, but also have to be aware of the changes that occur in their numbers.

Uncle Joshua Died Last Night is another game involving playing with words. The players are again seated in a circle. The leader says to his right hand neighbor, "Do you know that Uncle Joshua died last night?" The neighbor answers, "That's too bad. How did he die?" The leader answers, "With one eye shut," and shuts his eye.

The second player repeats the lines to the third and so on around the circle. All the players now have one eye shut. The first player then repeats the statements of Uncle Joshua's death and says "With one eye shut and his mouth awry." The third time he says, "With one eye shut, his mouth awry, and one foot held high." The fourth time around he adds "and waving goodbye." The group imitates and maintains all the descriptions made by the leader (until everyone succumbs to giggles!) .

A variation of Animal, Vegetable, or Mineral is Fish, Insect, or Bird. Any combination that seems appropriate for the group you are working with may be used. The first player says to the next player, "Animal." The second player must reply with an animal, such as a bear. The second player then asks the third player, "Fish, insect, or bird?" and continues through the group. If a child misses on his turn, he forfeits asking the question.

Because is a word game that focuses upon cause and effect relationships. The first child says, "The egg cracked." The second player gives a reason, for example, "I dropped it," while the third player must state the effect, for example, "It made a mess on the floor." Children should be encouraged to respond as rapidly as possible.

The ABC game can be played many ways. The leader states a category, such as cities, birds, fish, flowers, verbs, animals, or nouns. He then names a letter and chooses a player. The player must answer by the time the leader has counted to ten or is out of the game. If the player answers within the time limit, he names another letter and chooses another child to respond.

Alphabet Questions is played in a circle. The first player asks the second player a question about an object, animal, place, or plant in alphabetic sequence. For example, the question might be, "If I lived in Africa, what could I be?" The answering player could say, "I could be an ant." This player then asks the third player a question that uses the letter B, and so on through the alphabet.

In a variation of this game, the first player says, "I am going to California and I am going by F." The next player must name all the means of travel he can think of that begin with the letter F (freight train, fireboat, flying, and so on). Each child keeps score of the number of ways he can think up. This player then names the next place he is going to travel to, choosing his own letter. (Other variations may be used by the teacher to embody aspects of the curriculum such as history topics, science topics, and math concepts.)

The games described so far need a leader who can be chosen using the chants described earlier in the book. The next two games should be led by the adult in charge.

Fanny Dooley is a game that can have many variations. The leader is usually the only person who has the key to what is wanted. Each child tries to figure out the solution, but keeps it to himself until everyone has it figured out. Each child who does know what is wanted makes statements demonstrating his knowledge. For instance, the leader may say, "Fanny Dooley likes butter, but she doesn't like margarine; she likes cheese, but she doesn't like cream; she likes beer, but she doesn't like to drink; she doesn't like it cold, but she does like it freezing." The children must be able to come up with the fact that she likes things with double letters, but not single ones. This game can be used with specific letters of the alphabet, specific categories of objects, specific combinations of numbers, specific multiples of numbers, and so on.

Another game in this genre is Going on a Picnic. Here, the names of the things to be taken must begin with the first letter of the player's name, either the first or last.

This game may be varied to include specific categories, objects, places and.so on.

Which Ant? is a game that draws on the knowledge of word families. The leader asks a player, "Which ant has a long nose and big floppy ears?" The answer is a elephant. "Which ant was a general?" General Grant. Any word family may be used for this game. (For example, "Which *ice* is cut?" A slice. "Which *and* can be washed?" A hand.) The leader asks the second player a question. If this child can answer the question, he in turn asks the third player the next question, and so on. If a child is stumped, the questioner asks the fourth player the question.

Diagram 4: Hangman's Noose

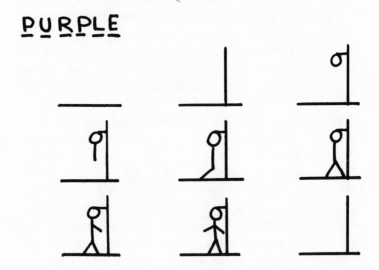

Hangman's Noose is a word game usually played by pairs of children. Paper and a pencil are required. The first child writes the first and last letters of a word on a piece of paper, marking with dashes the spaces for the missing letters of the word. The second child must guess the letters that are missing. Each time the child makes an error in guessing, a part of the hangman's noose is drawn (see diagram). When the body in the hangman's noose is complete (head, arms, legs, and torso), the game is over. This game can be played as a round-robin tournament.

Ghost is another game that draws upon spelling skills. Here, the child that goes first states the first letter of a word he is thinking of. The second child adds a letter. Each child adds a letter to spell a proper word. Rules at the beginning of the game could state that the word must be at least four or five letters long without the addition of "s." The player who either completes the word or gives an inappropriate letter gets a G, the first letter of the word *ghost*. A player may challenge any letter by asking the child who gave it the word he was thinking of. If the challenged child cannot give the word, he earns the G; if the challenger was incorrect, the challenger gets the G. The game is continued until a child gets all the letters in *GHOST*.

The last game in this series of games with words is called Guggenheim, which can be played with teams of about five children.

A chart must be made, like the one in diagram 5, a simple word, such as *cream*, written down the side. Five categories are listed along the top. The teams are given a time limit, such as ten minutes, in which to complete the grid. At the end of the time, each team tells the word it has in each category. If the word is used by more than one team, it is crossed out. Each team shares its words, crossing out those words that are duplicated and counting up those words that only they have used. The team with the most words is the winner of this game.

Dictionary is a game which, true to its name, involves the use of a dictionary. Here, the leader chooses a word

Diagram 5: Guggenheim

	ANIMALS	CITIES	NAMES	AUTHORS	COLORS
C	COW				CORAL
R	RHINOCEROS				RED
E		EVANSVILLE			
A				ALCOTT	
M			MELVIN		

that the children have probably never heard. Each child then writes down one definition of the word, only it must be written to sound like a dictionary definition. The leader reads all the definitions, including the actual one which the leader has written and included with the rest. As the leader reads each definition, he asks for a vote by the group as to whether or not they agree with the definition being read. At the conclusion of all the voting, the real definition is revealed.

10 Number Games

* * * * *

Number games do require facility with numerical operations. However, games seem to propel children to try, where serious work will turn them away. Although the number games presented below may be beyond the ability of the children you are working with, they could be presented within the context of fun.

In modern math, the use of magic squares is ubiquitous. Below are some different kinds of magic squares which call upon the use of addition.

In a three-by-three set of squares, the children have to arrange the numbers from one to nine in such a manner that the total in any direction is fifteen, horizontally, vertically, or diagonally. A five-by-five square can also be used with the numbers from one to twenty-five so as to make up a total of sixty-five in any direction.

Some number games fall within the realm of magic, which intrigues children and adults as well. Ask a child to think of a number; then ask him to double the number. When the child has completed this process he is asked to multiply by five and tell the result. In essence, the child is being asked to multiply a number by ten and remove the final zero, which leaves the original number intact (for example, 5 x 2 x 5 = 50, cross out the zero, leaving 5). Another magic trick in this genre requires the use of paper and pencil. One child asks another to write down numerically his birthday in month and days. For instance, if the child was born on May 4, the number would be 54 (5 because May is the fifth month, and 4 is the day). Then this number is multiplied by two giving in the example 108. Five is then added, yielding 113, which is then multiplied by 50, which gives 5650. To this number is added the child's age, which for the sake of the example we will set at 8, which gives 5658; 365 is then added to this, totaling 6023. The child who has done all this calculation hands the final total to the questioner. This child then subtracts 615 from 6023, giving 5408. This reveals that the child was born May 4th and is eight years old. Since the questioner supposedly does not know the birthdate of the first child the result will seem mysterious.

A long time ago, the Greeks were concerned with perfect numbers. Since then only seventeen perfect numbers have been uncovered. Most of the other numbers are either redundant or incomplete. But what does this all mean? To the Greeks, perfect numbers were those whose divisors added up to the number itself. The one they discovered was 6, whose divisors, 1, 2, and 3, add up to 6. The next one they found, 28, has the divisors 1, 2, 4, 7, and 14, which add up to 28. Other perfect numbers are 496 and 8128. That leaves thirteen more for the children to uncover. A number such as 18 is redundant, for its divisors 1, 2, 3, 6, and 9, add up to 21, while 16, whose divisors 1, 2, 4, and 8, add to only 15, is an incomplete number. Children can practice division and addition skills while looking for perfect numbers.

The 1089 trick can be played by a number of people at a time. The directions, using two different numbers as examples, will show how the game works.

	1	2
Write down a number with 3 figures	204	925
Write this number backwards	402	529
Subtract the smaller from the larger	198	396
Write this number backwards	891	693
Add the last two numbers	1089	1089

The number will usually be 1089. The children can try this with a variety of numbers, and discover which combinations lead to 1089 and which do not.

Have someone hide a dime in one hand and a penny in the other. Then ask him to multiply the value of the coin in his right hand by five and the value of the coin in his left hand by six. Then add the two obtained values and give the total. An odd total tells you the dime is in his right hand.

Throughout this set of magic tricks, addition, subtraction, multiplication, and division processes are practiced in a variety of ways that can be exciting because they are very different from the workbook exercises, which often become a "drag" to youngsters who need repetition. These games with numbers have play value for children. As I have emphasized throughout this book, sometimes it is play that teaches a child a skill more readily than schoolwork.

One of the first card games children can play is called Casino. In this game four cards are dealt to each of the players and four cards are placed face up on the table. At the beginning, a simple matching of cards takes place; the player with the most cards wins. As a child becomes more proficient, building and scoring can be added. A child can build with the cards numbered up to ten as long as he has a higher-value card in his hand. Even in this more complicated form of the game, the King, Queen, and Jack can be matched but cannot be built upon. In scoring, which a child should do, two points are given

for the ten of diamonds, one point for each ace, three points for all the other cards except for the two of spades which gets one point, and one point for the most spades. The winner of the game is the first to rack up twenty-five points.

Fan Tan is a game best suited to four players. A regular deck of cards is dealt out completely. The dealer starts the play by placing one of the four sevens on the table face up. If the dealer has no seven the next player starts. The suit can then be played out in order. Either the eight or six of the same suit is placed face up. A new suit can be started, in turn, whenever desired. The object of this game is to get rid of all one's cards before all the suits are completed.

11 Odds and Ends

* * * * *

Recent research has begun to support the notion that game playing has an impact on learning, and that in the long run, play, games, and cognitive development are functionally related. A recent study on the game Tick Tack Toe (Sutton-Smith and Avedon, 1971) indicated that those children who can win this game fairly consistently are different from those who consistently lose this elementary game of strategy. Winners tend to be better at arithmetic, to persevere at intellectual tasks, and to make more rapid decisions, whereas losers tend to be less independent, more dependent upon teachers and parents for approval, and more conventional intellectually. The researchers conclude that there are functional interrelationships between skills learned in games and other aspects of personality and cognitive functioning.

A series of games of strategy can be played with one, two, or more children. Many of these games must be purchased. These include Sorry, Parchesi, Stratego, and Dr. Nim.

Tick Tack Toe requires only a piece of paper, two pencils and two players. The object is to get a complete row of either circles or crosses in a line, horizontally, vertically or diagonally.

Another game of strategy requires a person knowledgeable in the tactics of the game. Usually an adult will have

Diagram 6: Towers of Hanoi

to handle this game until a child has caught on to the object of the game. Lay twenty-one small objects in a pile and invite a child to draw one, two, or three of the objects. The one who draws the last object loses the game. Whatever number of objects the child draws, you draw enough to total four. If the child draws three objects, you draw one; if the child draws two objects, you draw two objects, and so on. The child must draw the last object.

Dr. Nim works on the same principle. However, with this game, a child pits himself against the miniature computer inherent in the game. Within this game there are alternative strategies which can hold a child's interest for a long time.

The Towers of Hanoi is a strategy game for one player. If you do not purchase these towers, they can be made using eight circles of increasing size with holes drilled through them. A board with three dowels glued upright in holes drilled into the board needs to be constructed. The distance between the dowels should be the same and should allow room for the largest of the discs to be placed over each dowel (see diagram 6).

The object of the game is to move all the discs of the tower from one dowel to another, one at a time, with the smallest number of moves. Each move involves moving a disc from one dowel to another. There are two basic rules to this game: (1) only one disc is moved at a time and (2) a larger disc may not be put on a smaller disc.

Another paper and pencil game of strategy is called Boxes. Dots are made on a piece of paper like this:

```
.  .  .  .  .  .  .  .
.  .  .  .  .  .  .  .
.  .  .  .  .  .  .  .
.  .  .  .  .  .  .  .
.  .  .  .  .  .  .  .
.  .  .  .  .  .  .  .
.  .  .  .  .  .  .  .
.  .  .  .  .  .  .  .
```

Two or more children can play with the same grid at one time. Each child in turn connects two dots. The object is to make boxes for yourself while preventing the others from getting boxes. The child with the most boxes when the grid is completed wins the game.

Listening Games

The first game requires a small group of players. The first player says, "I packed Aunt Jemima's trunk with a calico dress." The next player repeats this and adds something new: "I packed Aunt Jemima's trunk with a calico dress and a shoe brush." The third player might say: "I packed Aunt Jemima's trunk with a calico dress and a shoe brush and a hat." Whoever fails to repeat the whole list and add a new item is out of the game.

Telephone, or Rumor, is another of the listening games. The children sit in a circle on the floor. The first child whispers something into the ear of the child to his left, who whispers it to his left-hand neighbor, and so on around the circle. The last child says the message he has heard aloud. By the time the message has gone around the circle it has been distorted in a variety of ways. The discussion afterwards about who has heard what can give clues as to where the breakdown has occurred.

Cat and Dog is another game that results in mix-ups. The leader hands an object to the child to his right stating, "I give to you a dog." The recipient asks, "A what?" The donor replies, "A dog." At the same time, the leader hands an object to the child at his left, stating, "I give to you a cat." The recipient asks, "A what?" And the donor answers, "A cat." This child passes the object to the next child stating, "I give to you ...." The recipient answers, and the donor turns to the leader saying, "A what?" The leader responds, the donor tells the recipient who then hands the object to the next player with "I give to you a cat" (or a dog, whichever the case may be), and so on around the circle. The fun begins as the children have to cross over the objects and confusion sets in.

Giant Steps is basically a listening game, but requires balance and locomotion skills. The players line up on a line twenty to forty feet away from the leader (who has been chosen by the group). The leader tells each child, in whatever order he chooses, how to move and in what ways to move. There are four ways in which a player can move: baby steps (the player puts one foot directly in front of the other, the back of the first foot touching the toes of the second foot); regular steps; giant steps (steps as long as the child can manage); and umbrella steps (where the child twirls in large circles). For example, the leader may says, "Susie, you may take three giant steps." Before Susie can move, she must ask, "May I?" and the leader must answer, "Yes, you may." Often the leader will say, "No you may not," and move on to another child or give another set of instructions, which must be inquired about again, according to the formula. If a child forgets to ask permission, that child has to go back to the starting line and begin again.

Red Light—Green Light is related to Giant Steps. A leader stands from twenty to forty feet away from the group. The leader turns his back and counts to ten while the group quietly creeps up toward the leader. When the leader reaches ten he shouts stop, at which point the players must freeze. If the leader sees anyone move, that child must go back to start. The leader turns his back and counts again. The players try to get close enough to the leader to tap him and then get back to the starting line before the leader can tap someone. The child who is tagged becomes the leader of the next round.

Watching Games

Changing Rhythms is a group game played with the children sitting in a circle. A child is chosen "It" and sent out of the room. A leader is determined by the group to do various motions, such as clap hands and snap fingers, which everyone in the group imitates. "It" is called back into the room and tries to guess who the leader is. The leader must change motions, but the group must follow quickly so that "It" has a hard time determining who the leader is.

Concentration is a game that draws heavily on visual memory. A deck of cards is laid out, face down, on a large table. Each player can turn over two cards in an attempt to make a pair. If a pair is made, the child gets to turn two more cards. This process continues until all the cards have been picked up. The child with the most pairs is the winner.

12 Theoretical Issues

* * * * *

Certain theoretical issues underlie the concept of learning disabilities. "Learning disabilities" is the latest term in a long list of labels designed, in part, to explain the lack of the development of reading skills in children. Such labels as laziness, willfulness, orneriness, mental retardation, and emotional disturbance have been applied previously. None of these have led to an understanding or to remediation of the problems. This latest of labels, learning disability, with its underpinning of some minimal brain dysfunction, once seemed promising. Recent research, however, has begun to discount the idea of dysfunction. Clements, in a 1966 publication of the U.S. Department of Health, Education and Welfare, defined the minimal brain dysfunction syndrome as a condition in "children of near average, average, or above average intelligence with certain learning or behavioral disabilities, ranging from mild to severe, which are associated with deviations of function of the central nervous system. These deviations may manifest themselves by various combinations of impairment in perception, conceptualization, language, memory, and control of attention, impulse, or motor function" (pp. 9-10).

The term "minimal brain dysfunction" has traveled under many pseudonyms that fall into two distinct types of nomenclature. One focuses upon possible organic factors, such as organic brain damage, cerebral dysfunction, and organic brain dysfunction. The second focuses upon the consequences, or behavioral after-effects, and includes such terms as dyslexia, primary reading retardation, and conceptual handicap.

By and large, there are four criteria used in the diagnosis of the minimal brain dysfunction syndrome: perceptual disorders, hyperactivity, conceptual disorders, and disorders of the thinking processes. Unfortunately these four symptoms do not clarify our understanding of learning disabilities as these are also symptoms of gross brain damage, mental retardation, and schizophrenia.

Labels may give us a sense of security, a way of lulling ourselves into believing that we understand what we are observing. However, new names do not solve problems. This brings us back to the problem of children who have difficulty learning, especially in reading.

Estimates of the incidence of scholastic difficulties range as high as forty percent, especially in the English-speaking countries where the language is not completely phonetic. Forty percent seems to be an unusually high figure. Reports from other countries around the world indicate a one to two percent incidence. If we accept the latter figure, then we need some further explanation to account for the other thirty-eight percent of our children who are in academic difficulty.

Thompson (1974) collected data from 1919 to 1970 on children who had suffered an attack of encephalitis. He states that he has not been able to find a single child who had learned to spell and read before the illness and had lost only these abilities after recovery. He did suggest that there is an alternative explanation. About ten percent of school-age children with reading disabilities, according to Thompson, exhibit a developmental lag. However, he says that early interventions can result in the development of adequate reading skills and cites such prominent examples as Thomas Edison, Albert Einstein, Woodrow Wilson, George Patton and August Rodin.

So far we have accounted for twelve percent of the children exhibiting reading disabilities. Of the remaining twenty-eight percent, approximately eight percent are children who have suffered recurrent ear infections during their preschool years. These infections interfered with the child's use of the auditory modality. Sometimes the child heard, sometimes not. Since the child could not depend upon the auditory modality, auditory input may well have been ignored. As such, language, which includes the written word, did not develop the degree of importance it did to the child whose hearing is not impaired intermittently. While this child can and often does learn to read, comprehension of the material seems to be seriously impaired. The remaining twenty percent of those with reading difficulties seem to have a variety of emotional problems.

While we may have but one cluster of symptoms affecting the reading process, we have many underlying causes. No matter what the etiology (brain damage, developmental lag, temporary hearing loss, or emotional difficulties), the ability to play, and thereby repeat, alter, and master everything that has made an impression on the child has been interrupted. The child is unable to solve the dilemmas he must face.

About fifteen years ago, White (1963) pointed out that theories of motivation (e.g. Hull and Freud) based on the action of primary drives were in trouble when they tried to explain behavior characterized as exploratory, playful, stimulus seeking, and novelty seeking. Ingenious work with concepts like "secondary reinforcement" or "countercathexis of instinctual impulses" have seemed to many to be clever verbal manipulations rather than convincing theories. White suggested that certain types of motivation do not require a source of energy external to the nervous system.

Although White did not elaborate on this point, the work on sensory deprivation (Zuckerman & Haber, 1965; Goldberger, 1966), sleep studies, and infant visual fixation tendencies (Berlyne, 1958; Fantz, 1961) clearly indicates that the human nervous system not only is in constant activity, but has a tendency to seek sensory input that contains novel components. Further, one may see in the play of children a tendency not only to seek sensory input but to create it. Perhaps the young child's preference for mother's pots and pans over the most interesting toys she can buy is partly due to the magnitude of the sensory input the child can create with them.

What are the opportunities that pots and pans offer? One can put things in them as well as take them out; one can pretend to be cooking. Put this pot on your head and it can become a helmet. You can put yourself into the pot (if it is large enough) and take yourself out of it. And then, of course, there is the alternative of using this marvelous equipment as a drum, which impinges, or has an effect, upon others.

The young child experiences a great deal of satisfaction from producing an effect as a result of his explorations. Piaget's observations (1952) document this particularly well. White calls the energies behind this type of behavior *effectance* and the effects of the doer's behavior upon the doer *feelings of efficacy*. This concern for the effect of one's action upon the environment, according to Piaget, begins during the third of his sensory-motor stages, at about four months of age. It can be seen that concerns about the effect of one's behavior on the environment, as well as attempts to maintain or repeat the behavior to hold onto the effects, begins early in life. According to White, it is this interaction with the environment, with the emphasis on producing effects and the use of developing skills, that leads to an accumulation of knowledge, and finally to *competence*.

Effects appear to be the motivation for continued exploration of the environment, continued development of skills, and continued creation of effects which are all bound into a sense of competence. The subjective experience of this process is accomplished by playing. What has been described so far is an active process, as it is only through continual interactions with the environment that an effect can be produced. For White, the whole notion of competence rests upon activity; it is through activity that a person learns, adapts, and grows. Learning, adaptation, and growth refer not only to the outside world, but also to the inner world of self. In essence, the child has to be able to test reality adequately and to find out who he is and what he can do and cannot do. This is the central task of middle childhood—the school years.

If we look at the typical first grader, we see that sense of excitement about school often revolves around learning how to read, for it is with the development of this skill that he begins to see his similarity to his parents most vividly. In addition, the child is learning from his peers which behaviors are appropriate and acceptable for his sex. The identification process is still going on beyond the age of five or six proposed by Freud, extending into middle childhood and beyond the relationship with parents.

In White's scheme, the process of identification, which extends into middle childhood, is tied up with feelings of competence. This process depends upon some elaboration and understanding of interpersonal relationships as well as one's role in the family. The child must be mature enough to be able to perceive the various roles employed in his family and, from there, to translate this knowledge into sociodramatic play, where he tries out the various roles. According to White (1963) the child who identifies with the adults in the environment does so because, by being like the competent model, the child strengthens his own feelings of competence.

In addition, the identification process is also a shortcut to the mastery of complex adult patterns of behavior. By imitating adult behavior, the child can try out various roles more quickly and effectively than by discovering them bit by bit. The development and struggles of the first five years of life come into focus during middle childhood, when the emphasis is upon the development of competence. In order to understand how the development of competence affects the child with learning disabilities based upon brain damage, let us return to the first two years of life.

During the first two years, the child's interactions with the world are primarily in a visual-motor mode. Although this modality has limits in terms of data gathering, the young child creates a vast storehouse of information in this sensory-motor manner. The child learns where he ends and the world begins; he begins to develop notions and understandings of himself in relationship to objects in the environment, and hence begins to develop a stable perceptual world where notions of space are experienced via the movement of his body through space. The difficulties a brain-damaged child encounters in establishing a stable perceptual world during this period of life eventually lead to learning disabilities.

The first system of relationships exists in the child's body via motor exploration, and is closely allied to the visual, auditory, and tactile modalities, as information is coming in through all the sense modalities concurrently. The child must match and gain the same information, at least through motor and visual modalities, for the system of relationships to grow. The child must learn to explore an object with his eyes in the same way he previously explored it with his body, for it is only by moving away from sensory-motor modalities to more cognitive ones that intelligence grows, and with it, the ability to conceptualize and to generalize.

Systems of relationships are developed by the child as a way of making sense of the perceptual world. Children also develop a system of relationships as a means of understanding interpersonal interactions. Failure in the conceptualization of perceptions will interfere with the understanding of interpersonal relationships. Consider, for example, the difficulty the "normal" young child has with the notion that grandparents are his parents' parents.

Confusion in the perceptual world, combined with confusion about interpersonal relationships and feelings of incompetence, can and often does lead to inappropriate behavior and poor reality testing. Taking this into consideration, one can hypothesize that the child will also be confused about the aversive responses he may receive from others in his environment, further emphasizing his feelings of incompetence and of unworthiness. Now we have the beginnings of emotional disturbance overlaying the original difficulties. Learning disabilities, then, cannot be treated only in terms of the perceptual and concomitant learning disabilities: all the areas need remediation.

An optometrist who specializes in perceptual training has suggested that he obtains the best results from those children who have been involved in psychotherapy concurrently with perceptual training. He felt that the growth of the children in the perceptual area stemmed from their greater awareness of their feelings and thoughts as well as their ability to distinguish between inner and outer reality. He also found that children with experience in psychotherapy respond more readily to spatial clues and internal promptings. They seem to have a better awareness of themselves as a whole, which helps in the remediation of learning disabilities.

Remediation of the weak perceptual and skills areas alone does not alleviate the feelings of incompetence the child has developed. On the other hand, psychotherapy alleviates neither the perceptual disability nor the learning difficulty.

The child with a maturational lag presents a different constellation of problems that contribute to feelings of worthlessness and incompetence, and eventuating in learning disabilities. Bender (1957) described these children as awkward in motor skills, impulse ridden, immature, and dependent.

First parents and other important adults and then teachers set up expectations for these children that they are unable to meet. We expect them to behave and function on a level appropriate for their age without a clear awareness of their inability to conform to our expectations. They fail not only in our eyes, but in their own as well, leaving them to feel ashamed of themselves.

Shame is one of the most painful feelings I can think of, with the most serious consequences for emotional growth. Shame is a heightened awareness of oneself, a feeling of being exposed and found wanting or defective in relationship to another person. It results in feelings of wanting to escape and hide. The interpersonal bridges between the child and the adult are temporarily broken as the child retreats into himself to repair the damage. Feeling ashamed can happen so automatically that the child may eventually avoid those activities that elicit that painful feeling (for example, school work). Then, on top of it all, the child may be yelled at or punished for those behaviors that are not appropriate for his age level, which once again adds to the child's feelings of shame. A vicious circle has been inadvertently started and often eventuates in a reading disability. The reading disability can reflect: (1) the child's inability to physiologically deal with the academic work due to the maturational lag; (2) the child's inability to deal with the academic work due to feelings of shame; (3) the child's anger toward those adults who have shamed him, which is reflected in a refusal to learn.

The child who has had ear infections during the preschool years, which have interfered with adequate hearing, has learned that he cannot depend upon the auditory modality. A phonic approach to reading leaves this type of child bewildered about the reading process. A sight-word approach offers this child a better chance to develop reading skills. In either case, this child has a great deal of difficulty understanding what he is reading just as he has had difficulty in communication with others due to misunderstanding throughout life.

Erikson (1968) has suggested that the child who has difficulty with language, which is a way of anchoring feelings and experience and a means whereby the child makes sense of them, has difficulty in exploring the environment adaptively. The sense of mastery over the environment and oneself is seriously inhibited. The child is unable to develop a sense of autonomy, a sense of himself as a separate and unique individual. The child fails to make sense not only of experiences and feelings, but also of interpersonal events as they occur. As a result, there is a great deal of misunderstanding in interpersonal situations. The child feels a distinct sense of powerlessness, which he fights, and which is expressed in a lack of compliance with authority in general. Another expression of this battle with adults is refusing to read. Here again is a vicious circle in the making.

There are many causes of emotional problems, some of which are parental mishandling, unusual and stressful life experience, and the child's own misunderstanding of experience. As the emotionally disturbed child gains help in understanding his problems in living, the reading problem tends to clear up, for the child has really been learning all along. He has not been able to use that learning effectively.

In addition to the various learning problems and attendant emotional difficulties, these children do not know how to play. The child with brain damage has difficulty focusing in on an object or experience for a long enough period of time. Much information is lost and consequently the play of the child is impoverished. Understanding and resolution of the problem being played out is also seriously impoverished. Alternatives cannot be entertained. The child is stuck in a repetitive play that leads nowhere. The child with a developmental lag, who has experienced shaming, becomes so inhibited that the playing out of problem situations is also inhibited. This child is afraid to act at all and hence does not play. He is trapped in the behavioral patterns that keep the vicious circle of shaming-withdrawal-anger-shame in motion.

The child with auditory problems receives so much contradictory information and has so many confusing experiences that he cannot sort them through, even in play. It is much easier to push these experiences aside rather than to attempt to deal with them. Play as a means of solving a variety of problems is ignored as a modality. Children with emotional problems are most likely to play. However, the repetitive play suggests that the child is stuck: he cannot generate alternative ways of looking at or solving the problem.

Psychotherapy seems to be helpful to these children. Children of this age are usually engaged in play therapy as the treatment modality of choice. It is through play therapy that children express their deepest concerns in a form they are unable to do verbally. In essence, the psychotherapist first has to teach children how to play, which has been one purpose of this book. Psychologists concerned with the development of children have for a long time functioned under the hypothesis that children who do not know how to play tend to be in serious emotional difficulties, for they are left helpless in the face of problems which they cannot solve. This is not to say that they can always solve their difficulties if they play, but there is more likelihood for this to happen when play is available. Toys that do nothing without the player are best; battery-operated toys are limited to what the toy can do by itself. Play gives children a feeling of active mastery which is needed not only for academic achievement, but also for work later on in life.

Games are one way of playing, make-believe another. Both are important for adequate development.

This book has focused upon the playing of games that were, once upon a time, taught by an older group of children to the younger group, so that the tradition was handed down from one generation of children to the next. The older generation of children is gone; there is only the younger generation to be taught. This book has been written mainly to jog the memories of the last generation to play games. It has not been designed to be an exhaustive study of all the games. More ideas can be generated by studying Peter Brueghel's painting *Children's Games*; he depicts over four hundred games that children have played over the centuries, in a variety of lands, under differing names.

My fantasy is that this book will provide a way for children to learn the games that once helped remediate deficits and encourage feelings of competence, help children assume responsibility for themselves, and encourage them to be active participants, and all learning disabilities will disappear forever. However, we may all wish too much too soon from the children we will be teaching the games to, and in the long run, lose sight of whatever gains they might be making. As was mentioned in the last chapter, as research has been done regarding the nature of the relationship between games and cognitive functioning, it has been found that games, playing, and learning are part of the same "family." One needs to keep this in mind as these techniques are tried. Good Luck.

Bibliography

CITED SOURCES

Bandura, A., and Walters, R. H. *Social Learning and Personality Development.* New York: Holt, Rinehart and Winston, 1963.

Bender, Lauretta. "Specific Reading Disability as a Maturational Lag." *Bulletin Orton Society* 1957, 1: 9–18.

Berlyne, D. E. "The Influence of Complexity and Novelty in Visual Figures on Orienting Responses." *J. Exp. Psychol.* 1958, 55: 289–296.

Clements, Sam D. *Minimal Brain Dysfunction in Children.* U.S. Department of Health, Education & Welfare, 1966.

Erikson, Erik. *Identity, Youth and Crisis.* New York: W. W. Norton & Co., 1968.

Frantz, R. L. "The Origin of Form Perception." *Sci. Amer.* 1961, 204: 66–73.

Goldberger, L. "The Interaction of Situational and Organismic Variables in the Effects of Perceptual Isolation." Paper read at the New York State Psychological Association meeting, May 1966.

Harlow, Harry and Zimmermann, Robert R. "Affectional Responses in the Infant Monkey." *Science* 1959, 130: 421–432.

Kephart, Newell C. "Perceptual Motor Aspects of Learning

Disabilities." In *Educating Children With Learning Disabilities*. Frierson and Barbe, Eds. New York: Appleton, Century, Crofts, 1967.

Moustakas, Clark. *Who Will Listen?* New York: Ballantine Books, 1975.

Piaget, Jean. *The Origins of Intelligence in Children*. New York: International Universities Press, 1952.

Redl, Fritz. *When We Deal With Children*. New York: Free Press, 1966.

Sutton-Smith, Brian and Avedon, Elliot N. *The Study of Games*. New York: John Wiley and Sons, 1971.

Thompson, Lloyd J., M.D. "Learning Disabilities: An Overview." In *Annual Progress in Child Psychiatry and Child Development*. Stella Chess and Alexander Thomas, Eds. New York: Brunner/Mazel, 1974.

White, Robert W. *Ego and Reality in Psychoanalytic Theory*. New York: International Universities Press, 1963.

Wolinsky, Gloria F. "Piaget's Theory of Perception: Insights for Educational Practices with Children Who Have Perceptual Difficulties." In *Educating Children With Learning Disabilities*. Frierson and Barbe, Eds. New York: Appleton, Century, Crofts, 1967.

Zuckerman, M. and Haber, Merry M. "Need for Stimulating as a Source of Stress Response to Perceptual Isolation." *J. Abn. Psychol.* 1965, 70: 371–377.

GAME SOURCES

Arnold, Arnold. *World Book of Children's Games*. New York: Crowell, 1972.

Hunter, J. A. H. *Fun with Figures*. New York: Dave Publications, 1956.

Morehead, Albert H., and Mott-Smith, Geoffrey. *Hoyles Rules of Games*. New York: New American Library, 1963.

Simon, William. *Mathematical Magic*. New York: Chas. Scribner's Sons, 1964.

Withers, Carl. *A Treasury of Games*. New York: Grosset & Dunlop, 1964.

Games have also come from unpublished sources and the memories of children and former children.

RECOMMENDED SOURCES

Almy, Millie. "Spontaneous Play: An Avenue for Intellectual Development." *Child Study*, 1966, 28 (2) : 215.

Freybery, J. "Increasing the Imagination Play of Urban Disadvantaged Children Through Systematic Training." In *The Child's World of Make-Believe*. J. Singer, ed. New York: Academic Press, 1973.

Gould, R. *Child Studies Through Fantasy*. New York: Quadrangle Books, 1972.

Klinger, E. *Structure and Functions of Fantasy*. New York: Wiley-Interscience, 1971.

Millar, S. *The Psychology of Play*. Baltimore: Penguin Books, 1968.

Piaget, J. *Play, Dreams and Imitation in Childhood*. New York: W. W. Norton & Co., 1951.

Piers, M. *Play and Development*. New York: W. W. Norton & Co., 1972.

Singer, J. *The Child's World of Make-Believe*. New York: Academic Press, 1973.

Smilansky, Sara. *The Effects of Sociodramatic Play on Disadvantaged Pre-School Children*. New York: John Wiley & Sons, 1968.

Sutton-Smith, Brian. "Piaget on Play: A Critique." *Psych. Review* 1966, 73 (1) : 104–110.

Valentine, C. W. *The Normal Child*. Baltimore: Penguin Books, 1956.

Index of Games